Long Memories
a memoir of Frank Belknap Long

Long Memories

Recollections of Frank Belknap Long

by

Peter Cannon

A British Fantasy Society
Publication

First published in Great Britain in 1997 by

The British Fantasy Society
2 Harwood Street
Stockport
SK4 1JJ

Designed, edited and produced by Peter Coleborn for
The British Fantasy Society

This publication © British Fantasy Society

BFS 002

ISBN 0-952-4153-1-3

British Library Cataloguing in Publication Data.
A catalogue record for this book is available
from the British Library.

Printed and bound in Great Britain by
Quacks the Booklet Printers
7 Grape Lane
Petergate
York YO1 2HU

"Long is my favourite 'adopted grandson' …
A great boy – & he'll never grow up!"

– HP Lovecraft, 1929

For my parents

Long Memories

Recollections of Frank Belknap Long

Contents

Introduction

I suspect not every Frank Long fan who reads this memoir will like it. Surely Frank himself, an intensely private individual, would not have approved. On the other hand, his wife Lyda, never one to shy from embarrassing personal revelations, may not have minded. They left no immediate survivors with feelings to consider. As only children who married too late in life to produce off-spring of their own, Frank and Lyda had to rely largely on friends to look after their needs in old age. I was one of those friends. In the absence of a son or nephew or grandson I played the part I did – and accumulated the experiences that form the basis of this booklet.

I originally thought I should first describe at some scholarly length the friendship between Frank Belknap Long and HP Lovecraft back in the 1920s and '30s. Then I imagined skipping across some four decades – those mysterious middle years that Frank neglected to cover in his *Autobiographical Memoir* – to the point where I myself enter the story. I would start out distant and detached, but as I became more and more personally involved lose my emotional grip, until I finally disintegrated, like one of Poe's mad narrators or Delapore at the climax of Lovecraft's 'The Rats in the Walls'. As a fictional technique this has a lot to recommend it, but in the end I decided it was unsuitable for a memoir, however gothic. A formal essay on FBL and HPL's relationship must await publication elsewhere.

In drawing on my memories of the Longs I have done some selecting and shaping, a bit of dramatizing if you will, but I have invented nothing. I have done my best to quote Frank and Lyda accurately.

As the epigraph for *Ackerley*, his biography of the British author JR Ackerley, Peter Parker quotes his subject from a letter to Stephen Spender: 'To speak the truth, I think that people *ought* to be upset, and if I had a paper I would upset them all the time; I think that life is so important and, in its workings, so upsetting, that nobody should be spared...' In the text Parker cites this passage in discussing *My Dog Tulip*, Ackerley's book about his Alsatian bitch, whose real name was Queenie. Ackerley acquired Queenie from her original owners through a fluke, and while she was a difficult and demanding animal, a trial to everyone who had to deal with her not least Ackerley himself, he remained devoted to her to the end. Parker notes: 'In celebrating Queenie Ackerley is celebrating life, in all its mess and muddle...' So I like to think in these pages I'm celebrating the lives of Frank and Lyda Long, both of whom incidentally were fond of dogs, in all their mess and muddle.

Peter Cannon

Prologue

They're here! It's too late I tell you!"

It was a little past seven on a pleasant July evening, and my fiancée and I were waiting, flowers and bottles of wine in hand, outside the apartment of legendary horror and science fiction writer Frank Belknap Long. It was his frail old man's voice we could hear through the door. That morning he and his wife Lyda had phoned to invite us to dinner. Just two weeks earlier I'd proposed to Julie. We'd recently returned from Massachusetts, where we'd announced our engagement to our respective parents. Now we were about to make another leap into the unknown. I'd considered not bringing my bride-to-be, but had decided it best to introduce her sooner rather than later to a side of my life that could be difficult. Having known Frank for years, I stood on the verge of entering the Longs' apartment as well as meeting Lyda in the flesh for the first time.

After further muffled bumpings and mutterings, the door finally opened. Lyda, in her wheelchair, welcomed us into a narrow hallway. A single overhead bulb illuminated blood red walls. Frank took the flowers and wine and disappeared into the darkness beyond. The rest of the apartment would remain in mystery, for it soon became clear that the party would be limited to the hall.

Despite her bad legs and her bulk, Lyda could maneuver well enough using her arms like an ape. At her bidding we sat down – she in a chair by the door, Julie in a chair next to her, and I in Lyda's wheelchair facing the ladies. Frank stood behind the wheelchair, hovering like Igor, as Julie later put it. From her vantage point she could observe him retreat at intervals, not always to apparent purpose, into the nether regions.

We declined a partly filled glass of vodka proffered by Lyda, instead accepting from Frank an empty, less than sanitary-looking glass, in which we poured vodka and orange juice. (Lyda's comment that neither of them was mechanical when we'd presented the wine suggested it was pointless to ask for a corkscrew.) Julie and I agreed to share the glass, counting on the alcohol to kill any germs. Frank mixed his vodka with Diet Coke, while Lyda swigged hers straight from the bottle. It was plain they'd been drinking before our arrival.

"What can I tell you?" Lyda began. But first she reached over and lifted Julie's turquoise-rimmed sunglasses off her forehead and put them on. After all she was the star that evening. "I'm being interviewed for *Interview*, Andy Warhol's magazine you know," she said. "Photographers have been over to take pictures of me, one in the bathtub."

What our hostess proceeded to tell us, with occasional prompting when she wearied or lost the thread, was the life story of Lyda Arco Long. Her parents were famous actors in the Yiddish theater in Russia. She caught polio when she was five so no stage career for Lydasha. From Russia they made their way to Shanghai, where she lived in a Catholic convent. At age fourteen or sixteen or twenty-one (her statements varied), she and her parents came to America. The family traveled through Canada in vaudeville. Her tone betrayed a certain disdain for Americans and, conversely, an elevated regard for Europeans.

"Don't take anything she says seriously," said Frank. "She's more American than I am, despite her criticisms of Americans." A native New Yorker, Frank owned that he spoke with a Brooklyn accent, though it struck me as being an old-fashioned, educated Brooklyn accent.

As a grown woman, Lyda continued, she had worked as an agent in New York. She had represented many prominent singers and musicians, including Myra Hess. She mentioned other names that were unfamiliar to me, though I had no reason to doubt the essential truth of her account, that she'd been active in the cultural life of New York from about the 1940s on and had known important people in the performing arts.

To substantiate her claim of past glory there was, screwed into the wall above us, a mural-like oil painting done in a flat, cartoon style. I was reminded of *New Yorker* magazine drawings of an earlier era. Several small isolated human figures stood out against a murky background, one of whom, a woman in elegant black dress and elaborately coifed red hair, was strangling a swan.

The Lyda Long of today was dressed in a two-toned pastel summer dress. "I made it myself," she said. "I never wear a bra." Her long gray hair was done up in an untidy bun.

As further proof of her cultured background, she sang for us – snatches of Russian folk songs and operatic airs. Hers was not only a strong but a trained voice. When she asked for requests, we suggested Cole Porter.

"Cole Porter? Who is this Cole Porter? Bah!" Cole Porter was evidently not part of her repertoire.

Lyda did allow 'Frankele', whom she ordered about like a servant, to share the stage briefly. He recited a couple of his own poems, most memorably the one with that portentous opening line, 'The gods are dead, the earth has covered them'. In addition, Frank produced a pen-and-ink drawing used as a logo for one of the World Fantasy Conventions. The design featured cameo portraits of those four giants of the genre: Edgar Allan Poe, HP Lovecraft, Stephen King, and Frank Belknap Long.

On one of his forays, after a few unsuccessful attempts to find them, Frank returned with Lyda's dark glasses. These flared at the tips in a pattern of black-and-white checks. Julie retrieved her less exotic pair.

With the business of the glasses sorted out, Frank could now serve dinner – deli food in plastic containers. We the guests ate tuna-fish salad with plastic forks while our hosts watched. They had already eaten, they explained. A dog that resembled a midget German shepherd wandered in, wearing a plastic necklace. The Hound of Tindalos? I had to lift the ice bucket off the floor to let the animal squeeze past the wheelchair. Cockroaches crawled on the painting of Lyda and the swan.

When Lyda resumed her narrative it was to hold forth on Frank.

"Don't take anything she says seriously," Frank piped up.

Lyda sounded serious enough on the subject of his 'orthopedist' father (in fact Frank Long, Sr., had been an orthodontist, a dental surgeon) and the decline of the Long family fortunes.

"For forty years Frank didn't have to do anything because of his family's wealth," she boomed. "He wrote a story only when he felt like it. Then somehow he found himself on welfare. Get it?"

Surely Frank had not been quite such a dilettante.

"When I first met Frank at a party, at the National Arts Club I think it was, I wasn't impressed. He was drunk and when he's drunk he drools. Then one Saturday night when I was lonely I called him up – I was one of those popular people everyone assumed had plenty of friends – and he was by himself too. That's where everything started. Get it?"

The time between their meeting and their wedding appeared to be only a matter of weeks.

"Once, when I first knew him, I was kissing him passionately and one of his teeth came out. Can you imagine, the son of a rich orthopedist, and he doesn't have a tooth to call his own in his head!"

"Are you happy, dear!" Frank shrieked from his post behind the wheelchair.

"He has to put gum in his mouth to simulate teeth!"

"Are you happy, dear, humiliating me in front of these people!"

"Frank is a child — that's why I married him," Lyda proclaimed triumphantly.

It may have been at this point that Lyda admitted she suffered from spells of manic depression. "It's genetic so drugs like lithium don't work," she said. "My mother had a lobotomy."

To our relief Lyda shifted her focus to me. She was impressed that I'd dedicated *Pulptime*, my novel narrated by the young Frank Belknap Long, to my grandparents. That's why she'd wanted to meet me. I must be a nice boy. When I told her my age – thirty-three – she couldn't believe it. I looked twenty-one. She herself was seventy-seven. She would get me on *Joe Franklin* to promote my book. Since Franklin was based in Secaucus I'd have to arrange for travel to New Jersey. She'd tried to phone me the night before and early that morning but had gotten no answer. When I confessed I'd spent the night at Julie's in Brooklyn, she smiled and exclaimed, "How un-Lovecraftian of you!" (She evidently knew Lovecraft had been a prude.)

Then it was my turn for a taste of the lash. "For a nice boy you're a cheapskate," Lyda declared. "You paid Frankele a measly twenty-five dollars for his introduction to your book."

I protested that I had paid him fifty dollars, then realized Frank may well have underestimated the sum deliberately when he told her about my offer. I defended my actions further by saying he was receiving a percentage of the royalties.

As if it were not already obvious, she admitted they had little money. They couldn't afford a maid. One problem was that Frank was such an innocent. Once she gave him a Russian brooch to go sell that was worth hundreds but he came home with only sixty dollars for it. Frank was so easily taken advantage of. He was like the title character of Dostoevsky's *The Idiot*.

Finally, around nine o'clock, Lyda wound down. "I've said all I have to say. Get it?" she announced. Our audience was over. Julie gave Lyda a kiss on the cheek and I kissed her hand in what I imagined might have been the Russian manner. We waved good-bye to Frank behind the wheelchair. I may have had a momentary pang about abandoning good wine they couldn't open (I'd had the foresight to bring red rather than white, in case refrigeration proved a problem), but decided not to delay our escape.

On the street, though we joked it was lucky neither of us had had to ask to use the bathroom, our mood was somber. So this was what married life could be like.

I

That memorable dinner proved to be the turning point in my relationship with the Longs. Before that night I considered Frank a casual friend. Afterwards, like it or not, I realized I had a bond with them both as demanding as any blood tie. Indeed, they were to occupy far more of my attention than my dedicatees, my two grandparents then living out their last years in California. Ten years earlier I'd observed Frank and Lyda at the fabled First World Fantasy Convention, two among a host of colorful characters who'd come to Providence, Rhode Island, HP Lovecraft's beloved home town, to honor the life and work of the great American horror writer. Ten years later, at Woodlawn Cemetery in the Bronx, I would scatter Lyda's ashes over Frank's grave.

To return to the beginning: I first set eyes on Frank around noon Saturday of Halloween weekend 1975. We were both registering late for the convention, in the lobby of the Providence Holiday Inn. The short, slight older man with wispy goatee picking up his program materials, if not immediately recognizable from youthful photographs I'd studied in Arkham House books, could be none other than – his name badge confirmed it – Frank Belknap Long. While I may not have felt exactly like the lady in that twenties song who danced with a man who danced with a woman who danced with the Prince of Wales, for a fan like myself to be standing inches from the person reputed to have been Lovecraft's best friend was no small thrill. Later that day and the next I lurked at the fringes while others paid court to this gentleman and a corpulent red-haired woman in a wheelchair by his side who I surmised was Mrs. Long. Only once did I overcome my diffidence. In the dealers room I'd picked up a copy of a fan magazine called *Xenophile*, a special Lovecraft issue filled with contributions from many of the writers present. 'Mr. Long', as I'm sure I addressed him, was kind enough to sign the page featuring his poem 'Innsmouth Revisited'. (I also got a friendly, self-deprecating fellow a generation older than myself named Ben Indick to sign his *Xenophile* article, 'Lovecraft's Ladies'.)

Sunday morning I was in the audience for the convention's final panel, 'Lovecraft the Man', whose participants included L Sprague de Camp, author of the controversial *Lovecraft: A Biography*; Dirk Mosig, a psychology professor acclaimed as the father of modern Lovecraft criticism; and Frank Belknap Long. Supported vigorously by Mosig, Frank did his best to rebut de Camp's image of the Providence Gentleman as impractical misfit and rabid racist. Most of us watching silently cheered these efforts. We felt de Camp had been too harsh, and in fact under pressure he would back down some – if not in front of his opponents on the panel then in print a year or so later. (What had provoked his undue severity, de Camp confessed, was impatience with weaknesses in Lovecraft he saw in himself.) More than once in his remarks Frank sorely regretted that his own book on HPL, *Howard Phillips Lovecraft: Dreamer on the Nightside*, which presented his case far better than he could in person, had not been ready by convention time.

A few months later, as soon as the order from Arkham House arrived, I devoured *Dreamer on the Nightside* as eagerly as I had de Camp's biography. Again, I was left dissatisfied, if for different reasons. De Camp at least presented a coherent, detailed account, however unsympathetic towards Lovecraft. While having a better understanding of his subject, Long was short on substance. After some charming vignettes in the early chapters, especially of HPL's courtship of his future wife, the memoir trailed off into rambling speculations and hypothetical conversations of little interest. Of course, Frank was writing forty to fifty years after events of which he'd kept no record. He'd simply forgotten much of the past and was too old and too tired to produce the kind of meaty reminiscence fans like me wanted, despite his keenness to correct de Camp.

In addition, Frank temperamentally was no biographer, either of himself or others. In 'Some Random Memories of HPL', his brief contribution to *Marginalia*, one of the early Arkham House volumes of Lovecraft miscellany, he warned his readers: 'Being in all respects the exact opposite of a Boswell, the most I can hope to do is put down for the record now, while my memories of Howard are still green, a few random impressions'. And a few random impressions they are indeed, among the poorest of the several personal tributes written by close friends in the decade following Lovecraft's death in 1937. (Without benefit of letters or other papers, W Paul Cook served HPL best in the Boswell role. His 'In Memoriam' is a magnificent effort, a model of its type.)

Here, too, I should admit that I was unimpressed by what of Frank's fiction I'd read, chiefly in the Arkham House collections of his stories and assorted paperback reprints. In my view Long was simply not in the same league as Lovecraft. How curious that his two most famous stories, 'The Space Eaters' and 'The Hounds of Tindalos', both written in the twenties, each used Lovecraft as their protagonist. (In the first tale, the narrator and his friend are called 'Frank' and 'Howard'. In the sequel, 'Frank' is still the narrator but, because he was killed off in 'The Space Eaters', the Lovecraft character returns as 'Halpin Chalmers' – who as before resides in 'Partridgeville', a name I always thought a bad choice for a New England town until I recognized it as a parody of 'Providence'.) Today these stories are notable as good-humored spoofs, not as sterling examples of weird fiction.

To be fair, Frank in his prime eschewed the weird or supernatural horror tale in favor of science fiction, a genre with a wider market. During the so-called Golden Age of Science Fiction, he shone as a star of the second or third magnitude – before fading with the pulp magazines that were fast becoming obsolete with the rise of the paperback. Not that he was without admirers among his peers. Ray Bradbury, to cite one distinguished name whose opinions deserve respect, has praised Frank's fiction for its gentle child-like wonder. Some readers still respond to this quality in his work, and no doubt future fans will be so affected. Alas, I cannot count myself among this elite. For me Frank's fiction remains at best competent, on average pedestrian, and at worst hilariously awful. I find him more naturally gifted as a poet than a prose stylist. In old age his reputation rested principally on his very survival, on his dedication for most of the century to a profession that paid him few rewards.

If unenthusiastic about the work, I was nonetheless interested in striking up an acquaintance with the man Lovecraft had regarded as his favorite 'adopted grandson'. In the summer of '75 I had moved from Massachusetts to Manhattan, to seek a career in book publishing. I was living on the Upper West Side, about a dozen blocks south of the West End Avenue address where Frank and his parents had made their home in the early and mid-twenties, when HPL had been a frequent caller. I was walking the same streets that Lovecraft and Long and others of their informal literary circle, the Kalem Club (so-called because the original members all had last names starting with 'K', 'L', or 'M'), had walked some fifty years before.

Dreamer on the Nightside, to its credit, did convey some sense of that magical era, with its long hours of carefree male companionship and genial conversation. Most of the Kalems were unhampered by regular jobs or wives. For Frank this must have been one of the happiest periods of his life. A slow recovery from an appendicitis, which had cut short his undergraduate studies at NYU, allowed him to read and write at his leisure. Encouraged by his mentor, who'd noticed his promise as an amateur journalist, he made his first story sales to *Weird Tales* magazine. For his older friend Howard, however, this period was a disaster. It had opened on high hopes with his move from Providence to Brooklyn in March of '24, to wed Sonia Greene, a fellow amateur who'd been pursuing him romantically since their meeting in June of '21 at a Boston convention. Economic and emotional difficulties soon put an intolerable strain on the marriage. It effectively ended in the spring of '26 when Lovecraft retreated home to New England, to spend his all too few remaining years, as he told one correspondent, in 'a dour celibate dignity'. In sum, Frank Long, last of the original Kalems, stood as a sort of living shrine that no Lovecraftian pilgrim to New York could afford to miss.

Finally, finding myself in Greenwich Village one lovely spring afternoon within easy walking distance of Frank's place on West 21st Street, I decided to pay him an unannounced call. I knew that he was at least aware of my existence, thanks to Dirk Mosig, who appeared to be in touch with everyone of consequence in the Lovecraft world. (At the Providence convention timidity hadn't prevented me from chatting with Mosig, with whom I'd since developed a steady correspondence.) Earlier in the day, at the Science Fiction Shop, then located on Eighth Avenue, I'd bought a less than pristine copy of *Marginalia* – for eighty dollars. A hefty price perhaps, but the rare and long out-of-print *Marginalia* was an essential volume for one's Lovecraft library and, it occurred to me as I left the SF Shop, potentially something of interest to Lovecraft's best friend.

Frank lived in Chelsea, a neighborhood north of the Village that had seen better days but was starting to revive. His block, between Ninth and Tenth Avenues, was a pleasant tree-lined street, occupied for much of its southern length by General Theological Seminary (Episcopal). His address, 421, proved to be a brick building six stories high, with gardens at either side of the entrance, a pair of heavy glass doors. Inside a short flight of steps led up to a glass-fronted door. A lace curtain hid the lobby area beyond. I pressed the buzzer for 1-A, 'Long-Arco'. It appeared the Longs lived on the ground floor. Arco, I later learned, was Lyda's maiden name.

I identified myself over the intercom and after a minute or two Frank appeared at the curtained door, dressed in a plain brown bathrobe. I don't remember whether we shook hands. Probably not. If so it was the first and last time. Frank was not a person who invited such physical familiarity. While I explained how Dirk Mosig had suggested I look him up, Frank nodded. As a conversation starter, I showed him my recent purchase. "Oh, yes," he said, perking up, "one of Howard's first Arkham House books." (He quaintly pronounced it 'Awkum'.) "I paid $3.50 or thereabouts for it when it came out. Now I'd say a copy without the jacket like yours there would fetch as high as thirty-five or forty dollars…" After a pause Frank explained that he was halfway through writing a novel to order for a paperback house, and since it was due in thirty-six hours he had to get back to it. In any case, his wife wasn't feeling well. We parted with assurances we'd meet again soon.

After this encounter I was in no mood to take any further initiative to get together with Frank. A shy man with important work to do, he didn't need yet another stranger pestering him about the past. What, after all, did I have to offer in return? Over the next few years I saw him only on occasion, in the company of other fans, most of whom like myself belonged to the Esoteric Order of Dagon or EOD, an amateur press association whose members self-published 'zines' devoted in theory to matters Lovecraftian. These outings afforded little chance for increased intimacy because Frank's voice was so hard to hear. (No doubt a set of false teeth would have helped.) In a group of any size you had to be sitting right next to him to catch everything he said and somehow I never was. Conversation could be awkward in any event, with long pauses while Frank puffed on his ubiquitous pipe. During one such gathering, in the fall of '79, though, I did manage to get him to inscribe my copy of *Dreamer on the Nightside*.

At this time I had only a dim notion of Frank's financial situation. That he might be truly short of funds finally came home to me in a little incident a year later at the Sixth World Fantasy Convention, held outside Baltimore, Maryland. That Sunday morning of the convention weekend, after discovering the hotel dining room offered only a pricey brunch, I decided to opt instead for breakfast in the snack bar. There I was surprised to pass Frank on his way out, carrying a hot dog.

II

Then again, maybe Frank always ate hot dogs for breakfast. At any rate, for him I'm sure I was just another vaguely familiar face in the convention crowd, while for me there were other senior figures on hand of fresher appeal. Most memorably I stood in a decaying Baltimore graveyard at midnight while Fritz Leiber, who'd corresponded with Lovecraft in the final months of his life, recited Poe's 'Conqueror Worm' and 'The City in the Sea'. Earlier in the day I listened to a panel of such younger heavyweights as Stephen King and Peter Straub discuss trends in fantasy and horror in the eighties. I pricked up my ears when the conversation turned to the use of HP Lovecraft as a fictional character. Rumor had it that a novel about HPL was in the works.

This was both exciting and unsettling news. For some time I'd been contemplating writing an extended story with Lovecraft as hero, and I feared that another person had already thought of my particular twist – juxtaposing him with Sherlock Holmes. Since the success of Nicholas Meyer's *The Seven-Per-Cent Solution* in 1974, there'd been a spate of novels wherein the great fictional detective dueled with this or that historical personage (or other fictional character, like Dracula). As far as I knew no one yet had thought of linking him to Lovecraft, but I felt that I'd better get cracking before somebody else did.

On the other hand, Lovecraft was not as obvious a candidate for such treatment as, say, Oscar Wilde or Lewis Carroll, given his birth date of 1890. To have Holmes enlist HPL's aid in a case the detective would have to be on the elderly side – and, if I was to retain some vestige of verisimilitude, he would have to be the one to cross the Atlantic since the horror writer never set foot outside North America. ('I must see London, Child, before I die', Lovecraft once wrote Frank, but he was too poor ever to afford the trip.) I also had to think of a strong motive to bring Holmes to the USA after he'd long retired to the Sussex Downs to raise bees. And what of Watson? Well, the good doctor wasn't indispensable. For the role of narrator I had in mind a character who was as close a friend and disciple to Lovecraft as Watson was to Holmes – the young Frank Belknap Long. The rest of the Kalems – for it was in the heyday of the Kalem Club that I decided to set my apocryphal adventure – could lend background support, like the Baker Street Irregulars whose services the detective from time to time employed.

The following February I began the first draft. About a year later I had a finished manuscript of short-novel length. My friend Ted Klein, editor of *Twilight Zone* magazine, suggested I call it *Pulptime*, to echo EL Doctorow's *Ragtime*, which likewise mixed fictional with real people, among them Harry Houdini. The famed escape artist and anti-spiritualist campaigner had a key part in my story as well. Before starting the search for a publisher, I knew I had to secure Frank's permission to proceed. As a book editor I was aware that as a rule you avoided putting living people into a work of fiction, unless thoroughly disguised. I was hopeful, however, that Frank would find nothing offensive in my portrait of him as a young man, indeed might even give the project his blessing. I considered requesting permission through Frank's agent, Kirby McCauley, but on Ted's advice I simply sent him the manuscript directly and waited nervously for his reaction. I agreed with Ted it was better not to raise the permissions issue immediately.

A couple of weeks later Frank called, from the street. Evidently he had no phone. It appeared he liked the story, but I'd gotten a few things wrong. Morton and Leeds, for example, two of the Kalems, never used slang in their speech as I had them do. It was his mother who had been the oversolicitous one, not both parents. And so on. I promised to emend the narrative accordingly. Furthermore, I assured him I hadn't submitted the manuscript anywhere, nor was I trying to pass it off as his work. Frank was especially concerned that he not be credited as author. Then he spoke of his personal situation:

"It's been a terrible year for me. My wife's had an operation, I'm behind in my work, I haven't had time to socialize, not even with Tom." Tom Collins, a fellow EOD member, lived in Frank's neighborhood and was, I gathered, his closest friend. "But I do want to go over the manuscript with you. I'll call you again in two weeks. We can meet at a local bar."

When in closing I said I was willing to let him have a share of any income from the sale of *Pulptime*, he replied, "Don't worry about that."

I waited a month for Frank to phone back before initiating a get-together of the New York area gang. I hesitated to be too direct. In the end the only EODer available was Tom. A few days before the June date Tom and I had set, I mailed Frank a postcard inviting him to join us for dinner, our treat. Tom later confirmed that Frank could make it but only for the early part of the evening. His wife was too ill to leave alone for long. Later that night Tom and I would attend an off-off-Broadway play with a plot inspired by Poe.

When at six o'clock that Saturday I arrived at our designated rendezvous spot, a Blimpie's on Eighth Avenue, the two of them were already seated. "I was just telling Tom about your story," said Frank. "How you got the slang all wrong." He went on to say he didn't think Arkham House would be a good place to submit *Pulptime*. He didn't explain why, or else his remarks were lost in the background noise.

At Tom's suggestion we left the Blimpie's for a bar a couple of blocks away. It was drizzling and Frank walked slowly, though for a man of around eighty he seemed in pretty good shape, both physically and mentally. The only obvious sign of decay was his tobacco-stained fingers. We stopped briefly at Tom's so Frank could use the bathroom. I remained in the hall outside the apartment – Tom hoped I wouldn't mind but it was too much of a mess. "My place isn't fit for visitors either," Frank added.

We passed Frank's building on West 21st, and again I noted that he lived on an attractive block. At a trendy restaurant on Tenth Avenue we got a table in the bar area and ordered drinks – beers for Frank and myself, a Scotch for Tom. While Tom did most of the talking, I did get a chance, for the first time, to ask Frank about himself. He'd spent all his life in New York, his first home having been in Harlem, where he was born. He didn't especially care for the city, though. In fact, like Lovecraft, he preferred New England. During the summer he and his wife got away to the country. (Perhaps they weren't so badly off, I thought.) He was pleased with Tom's interview of himself in *Twilight Zone*, which I'd read in a recent issue. Tom smiled. Unlike myself, he was at ease with Frank, to the point of engaging him in a little playful kidding.

HPL had been a tremendous letter-writer, Frank resumed, but he less so. "I'm very careful about what I say in letters," he said, confessing that he'd been burned by being too candid in writing to Donald Wandrei, one of the founders of Arkham House, concerning a certain notorious figure in the Lovecraft world. As for the volume of mail he received, "I have more correspondents than I can possibly handle – professors and fans asking about Lovecraft and so forth. I don't have time to answer them."

Frank appeared to take a more balanced view of his late friend's literary stature than the run of his correspondents. "Joshi exaggerates HPL's greatness," he said. "He's not Henry James." Frank was referring to leading Lovecraft scholar ST Joshi, whose last name he pronounced '*Jaw*-shi' instead of '*Joe*-shi'. Though he would hear others say it correctly, he never would get it right. Back in the thirties Frank had called a new member of their circle, Herman C Koenig, '*Co*-nig' instead of the proper '*Kay*-nig'. In a letter from this period Lovecraft remarked, 'Belknap – who is slow to learn new ways – still says Co'nig quite unashamedly!'

A little before eight Tom and I announced we had to go if we were to get any dinner before our play started. Tom picked up the tab – one beer for Frank, two beers for me, and two Scotches for himself. On the sidewalk we said good-bye. For the moment the rain had stopped. "I'll write you with my comments and suggestions for your story," Frank assured me before heading home.

Tom and I grabbed a hurried bite at a Chinese restaurant across the street. *Extraordinary Histories*, a mishmash of various poems and stories, turned out to be enjoyable enough, though the non-Poe fan would have been mystified. I parted from Tom afterwards with promises of trying to arrange an EOD expedition to the Bronx to visit the Poe Cottage, which HPL and Frank and others of the Kalems had toured some sixty years before. But Tom was soon to leave New York for a job on the West Coast and no trip to the Poe Cottage materialized that summer.

Neither did any communication from Frank. I sent *Pulptime* to Jim Turner, editor of Arkham House, who in rejecting it confided that they already had a novel with Lovecraft as a major character under contract. So the rumors were true. At least this other book, judging from Jim's remarks, didn't also feature Sherlock Holmes.

At the World Fantasy Convention that fall, held in New Haven, I spotted Frank and Lyda but made no approach. Three weeks later a group of us made one of our Saturday tours of the Village bookstores, from the Strand and Forbidden Planet in the east to Foul Play and the Science Fiction Shop in the west. Though no one had tried to alert him in advance, a tentative part of our itinerary included dropping in on Frank.

Since I'd forgotten to check his address before leaving in the morning, it took us some searching to find his building that afternoon. Lyda responded to the buzzer and after a bit of a wait Frank appeared at the door. He seemed quite pleased to see us, indeed went on to say how disappointed he'd been to see no EOD people in New Haven. He'd been taking a nap and could join us in twenty minutes. "I was going to call you," he said to me.

At my suggestion we wandered over to the Blimpie's on Eighth. The gang was content to pass on visiting the Nicholas Roerich Museum, which housed a collection of paintings that had deeply impressed Lovecraft half a century before. Once settled, Bob Price and I returned at a leisurely pace to West 21st Street to retrieve Frank. Back at the Blimpie's I bought him a cup of coffee. Again, because there were five of us in addition to Frank, it was a challenge to catch his every word. He'd brought a number of items to show us – Spanish and Italian editions of his tales, translations of the usual Long classics, as well as copies of a new story in chapbook form, *Rehearsal Night*. I accepted Frank's offer to purchase one of these, with its tobacco-smudged cover, for the bargain price of twelve bucks. It regularly cost fifteen.

"I'd like to see a 'best of' collection of my stories. No one's done it yet," Frank said. He admitted Lester Del Rey had been an enemy since some long ago dispute so there was no hope for the Del Rey paperback line. "I've written some of my best stories in recent years, yet *Twilight Zone* keeps rejecting them. Not cheerful enough, I suppose." In fact, Ted had published a new tale of his to accompany Tom's interview, but I could see how from his perspective that didn't really count.

Bob solicited Frank to contribute to his zine, *Crypt of Cthulhu* (subtitled 'A Pulp Thriller and Theological Journal'), which was beginning to circulate outside the EOD. A Baptist minister as well as community college teacher, Bob was an enterprising fellow with a good sense of humor. In particular he hoped Frank would be willing to compose a passage from the *Necronomicon*, Lovecraft's mythical tome. Evidently there was more demand for new Long fiction at the fan than at the professional level.

Frank wrote ST Joshi a check for ten dollars, payment for some obscure item or service ST had provided. "My bank is closed," he said. Using the cash I'd given him for the chapbook didn't seem to be an option. When someone asked whether the accent on the word *Tindalos* fell on the first or second syllable, he chuckled and said he didn't know. Either pronunciation was correct.

Finally, Frank expressed astonishment at the sexual explicitness of *Penthouse* and other skin magazines of the modern era. "Such things would've been unimaginable when I was growing up. Absolutely unimaginable." Where had Frank seen *Penthouse*, I wondered Courtesy of some obliging fan?

A few days later I read *Rehearsal Night*. A total muddle. If it was representative of his recent work then, as Ted had suggested, the 'early Long' was synonymous with the 'best of Long'.

III

In early February of '83 Frank called from a pay phone – in the rain, no doubt. He had several questions to ask me. Had I heard from Tom? Not since Christmas, I replied. Was I in touch with Marc? Marc Michaud, publisher of Necronomicon Press, had given him an advance to write an autobiography and he was late delivering the manuscript. Based in Rhode Island, Necronomicon specialized in Lovecraft-related books and magazines, including the scholarly journal *Lovecraft Studies*, edited by ST Joshi. I told Frank not to worry, Marc could wait a little longer. Finally, who were those other two guys, besides Bob and Joshi, at the Blimpie's last fall? I could remember the name of only one of them myself. Frank stopped talking once his three minutes were up.

Clearly our visit had meant a lot to him. Feeling guilty, I phoned Ted and said I thought Frank would appreciate having some company. Ted confessed he hadn't gotten in touch as he'd mentioned he would, but would drop him a line the next day. A month later the two of us and Alice, an editor friend of Ted's, had dinner with Frank at Harvey's, an old-fashioned, wood-paneled restaurant that was a Chelsea landmark and a nice change from Blimpie's. Beforehand I met Frank at his building. On the walk over he launched into his litany about how many letters he received from fans and scholars and how he regretted having time only to answer a few. He was amazed at how much money some horror writers were being paid. Over dinner I sat at the opposite end of the table, next to Alice. Ted had the task of making conversation with Frank. Afterwards Ted and I agreed that for someone billed as Lovecraft's 'best friend' Frank simply wasn't that interesting. What had Lovecraft found so fascinating? (In fact, when I studied HPL's *Selected Letters* carefully, I saw that he grew progressively disillusioned with his young protégé.)

In June Frank phoned me to say he'd enjoyed my 'interview' with Lovecraft in the latest *Twilight Zone*. "You got HPL's speech just right." No great feat, as I'd constructed the text from passages in Lovecraft's letters. As usual he hadn't heard in a while from Tom. He had a story appearing in an anthology, *Whispers 4* (actually *Weird Tales 4*, I later learned, a less prestigious venue), and was working on a novel. "It's gratifying to receive all the kind letters from people, especially in the last year or two," he said, "but unfortunately that doesn't translate into increased income."

Early one morning toward the end of July Frank called to ask to borrow twenty dollars. He needed it to get through the weekend. Normally his agent took care of tiding him over, but Kirby was out of town. He met me later at my office, which, located at Park and 32nd, wasn't too far to come from Chelsea. Frank gave me a check. I promised not to cash it until the following week, presumably after the deposit of his monthly Social Security check. "My wife is difficult," he explained. "She thinks I have a much larger income than I do."

Two weeks later I had lined up Bob and Sam (one of the guys at the Blimpie's Frank had been curious about) for another social outing. Frank was ready for us when we arrived at his door. At his suggestion we walked over to a diner on the corner of Ninth and 23rd, the Chelsea Square. He'd had another place in mind that might have been a little nicer, but the Chelsea Square turned out to be perfectly decent.

Frank said he was pleased with the ten dollars Bob had paid him for his three-hundred-word extract from the *Necronomicon*. "I put in two hours work on it." Five dollars an hour didn't strike me as a very good rate. Bob offered to pay him forty dollars for a sequel to 'The

Hounds of Tindalos'. Frank said he'd do it right away since he needed the money. "In the past couple of years I've received all sorts of awards," he added. "Isaac Asimov gave me a silver cup. But they don't translate into cash." Frank then got going on Stephen King, who was fast becoming the most commercially successful horror author of all time. Frank just couldn't understand it. Why was Stephen King, also a client of Kirby's, raking in the millions while he wasn't?

Frank admitted to writing pornographic novels in the past. These apparently hadn't been anymore of a goldmine than his legitimate fiction.

Frank tended to repeat the same themes. Now and then, though, he'd come up with a new Lovecraft anecdote. This time he mentioned that the two of them once climbed up on a New York lightboat where Howard recited his narrative poem 'Psychopompos'. This was the sort of detail we fans wished he'd put more of into *Dreamer on the Nightside*.

When Frank complained that the publisher of *Weird Tales 4* hadn't sent him his contributor's copies, Sam gave him his copy, which he'd bought earlier in the day. (I later read Frank's story, 'Homecoming', in which Lin Carter, the series editor, had let pass the howler, 'The letter had clearly been written before his uncle's death,' the letter's author being the uncle.) At parting Frank told me he'd like to get together again with *'Twilight Zone'*, meaning Ted. I said I'd see what I could arrange, but their meeting at Harvey's proved to be their last before Ted resigned the magazine's editorship in 1985.

In early December I received a rejection letter from Pinnacle, the one professional house where I felt I had a prayer. The editor had held *Pulptime* for months, but in the end decided it was aimed at too specialized a market. That same day, however, a letter came from W Paul Ganley, editor of Weirdbook Press, a specialty publisher I'd queried, asking to see the complete manuscript. By New Year's Ganley had sent me his acceptance. I had agreed to change the ending – and to try to persuade Frank to provide a foreword.

In late January I met Frank after work at his building. This time he let me into the lobby area, while he returned inside his apartment. Ten minutes later we were on our way to the Chelsea Square, where we had dinner. "My wife doesn't like it here. Not fancy enough for her." In fact the food was good and reasonably priced. "She gives me a hard time sometimes," he added. As usual Frank lamented his not making any money from the attention he'd been getting. "I'd like to see a collection of my later stories published, my best stories, but there doesn't seem to be much of a chance of that. I've been able to place nearly all my stories in the past couple of years, through Kirby, and there may be a television sale in the offing. The money, though, is in novels. I'm working on two of them now." The vagaries of literary reputation concerned him. He was astonished that Joseph Hergesheimer, a well-known writer in the twenties, could be so utterly forgotten today.

At last I broached the subject of his writing a foreword to *Pulptime*. I said I could get him fifty dollars, apparently his minimum rate, plus a one-percent royalty. Ganley had given me a hundred-dollar advance – *Pulptime* was not going to make either my fortune or Frank's. I said I'd changed the story so that now it was his mother, not both his parents, who worried overly much about his health. To my relief, Frank was agreeable. He'd do it right away. His main concern was that he be paid up front. As for content: "Maybe I'll have some news about hearing from Sherlock Holmes."

Frank had recently heard from another one of Lovecraft's 'grandsons', Alfred Galpin, who was in Paris. Galpin had just sold his Lovecraft letters. Frank had sold his Lovecraft letters long ago to Samuel Loveman, another friend of HPL's, for hundreds of dollars when his mother was sick and he needed money to pay her hospital bills. "If I'd held on to them they'd now be worth tens of thousands." It irked him that old letters of his were being sold and he got nothing. Some years after HPL's death, Loveman had turned against Lovecraft after reading anti-Semitic comments in letters to others. In his friend's defense, Frank said Howard got along well with Sonia's Jewish friends, including a noted columnist named Isaacson. On the other hand, Mosig went too far, was too fanatical in trying to clear Lovecraft of the racist charge.

When I commented on the bond between himself and HPL, Frank confirmed it: "Howard very much saw a younger version of himself in me. We both came from similar old American families, we both had coddling mothers." In his youth Frank was an agnostic, much to his mother's distress. Mrs. Long had been a regular churchgoer.

On the walk back to his door Frank said he'd had a letter recently from Joseph Payne Brennan, another *Weird Tales* veteran. Brennan had a heart condition, while his wife had suffered a nervous breakdown. His latest short story collection, even with the Stephen King introduction, evidently didn't sell much. "So relative to others, I'm not doing so badly," he said.

As soon as I got home I wrote Frank a note thanking him for his cooperation and enclosed a check for fifty dollars. A few days later he phoned to thank me. "Fifty dollars is fine," he said. "You needn't bother about a royalty or a contract."

IV

A s a junior editor at a major New York publishing house, however, I did care about such formalities. In due course Paul prepared a letter agreement for Frank that permitted me to use the persona of his younger self as *Pulptime*'s narrator in return for a fifty-dollar flat fee and a one-percent royalty on any reprint.

In late February Frank phoned to tell me he'd almost finished his foreword, or introduction as he called it, to my book. "I want to read it over another time before mailing it to you." It sounded as if I'd have it shortly. He was still anxious about the status of his autobiography. He was supposed to get $150 on delivery of the manuscript, having already received three hundred dollars. This struck me as big money for Necronomicon Press. He hoped to take a week off to clean up the apartment so he and Lyda could have friends over. He indicated he'd enjoyed the most recent New Kalem gathering, which I'd missed.

For about a year, in emulation of the original Kalem Club, some of us Lovecraft devotees had been meeting regularly at the East Side apartment of Lin Carter, another senior horror-fantasy figure. With his slight build, thick-lensed glasses, gray mane of hair and goatee, Carter could have been taken for Frank's younger brother (a more worldly and profane younger brother, I hasten to add, for our bachelor host, who liked to boast of his male prowess, favored the erotic in his decor – most memorably cartoon drawings in his bathroom of sexually active aliens). Frank was always welcome to join the group, but because it was a long way to go and Lyda was ill he invariably failed to appear, until the one time I happened not to be present.

A few days after our phone conversation, at the next New Kalem meeting, I asked how the previous one had gone with Frank there. Bob said Frank had had a good time but had nodded off after one glass of wine. Bob was contemplating a special Long issue of *Crypt*, to include a couple of unreprinted stories from the twenties, 'The Eye Above the Mantel' and 'The Desert Lich'. On the question of the early versus the late Long, Lin was blunt: "Frank's a terrible writer. Always has been. He's a sweet old guy, though."

Three weeks later, en route to another gathering of the New Kalems, I decided to swing through Frank's neighborhood and was lucky enough to run into him on West 21st Street. "I was just on my way to the phone booth on the corner to call you," he said. Lyda had been sick, with edema, and might have to go into the hospital again. "There past two months I've never been under such pressure." They hoped if she was healthy enough to make it to the forthcoming Lunacon in New Jersey, where they could see friends. He hadn't had a chance to straighten up the apartment. As for the introduction to my story, he had revised it and made it much stronger since he'd promised he almost had it ready. He had only the last paragraph to work on. He'd mail it to me soon. "I doubt I'll make it this afternoon, but please give everyone my greetings." At the New Kalem meeting, Lin did a wicked imitation of Frank mumbling then falling asleep on the couch.

More than a week later Frank called: "I've just put my introduction for you in the mail. It runs to five pages, part of it handwritten because one of my typewriters broke down." He had both a pica and an elite, he explained. He'd tried to keep the piece light as befitted the tone of the story, which he recognized was basically a comedy with some serious bits. Lyda was still in the hospital, but was doing okay and might be out by the end of the week. He didn't get to the Lunacon – too far to go, especially on St. Patrick's Day and with uncertain travel arrangements at the other end.

Two days later it came – four untidy sheets, mostly typed, with the final page in blue ink. Notwithstanding the agonizing wait, I had no reason to complain. How often does an author get his narrator to supply a foreword? The spirit was appropriately tongue-in-cheek, though Frank couldn't resist a pessimistic aside when touching on the subject of Lovecraft's fame enduring well into the twenty-first century: 'always remembering, of course, that there may not be a twenty-first century for Man'.

After sending him a note thanking him for his foreword, he phoned to say he was glad I liked it. He'd sent the letter agreement back to Ganley. At the next gang gathering I got everyone to sign a birthday card to Frank. In my note I suggested we meet soon for dinner. He called on his birthday, April 27. "Have you heard from Crawford?" he asked. By Crawford he meant Ganley. (He probably was confusing Paul Ganley with William Crawford, a small press publisher who'd issued HPL's 'The Shadow over Innsmouth' in book form in the thirties.) I gave him an update on the status of *Pulptime*, which was scheduled to come out in the summer. Lyda was again in the hospital. "This year has been terrible," he said. "I've never been under such pressure." The usual refrain. He was curious to find out how I knew it was his birthday. I said I'd seen it in a who's who of fantasy. He promised to call another time to schedule a get-together.

As the publication date neared, I had a scare when I discovered that Sherlock Holmes was not in the public domain and I would need permission from the estate. I was fortunate that the estate's US representative and I were quickly able to come to an understanding.

Frank and I spoke again in June. Lyda was in and out of the hospital. He hadn't finished his novel, which Kirby was sure he could sell, despite the field not being in very good shape for the past couple of years. I informed Frank that the New Kalems were no more, since Lin Carter had been evicted from his apartment. (Serious financial and health problems would take their toll on Lin, who was to die in 1988.) In another conversation he reported he was under too much pressure to set a date to get together. Lyda had been difficult. "When she's feeling well she gets angry and takes it out on me," he confided. He worried about the cost of a phone call going up to twenty-five cents. "Lyda makes a lot of them." In discussing *Pulptime*, he continued to refer to Ganley as 'Crawford'.

The last week of July he called to borrow thirty dollars. For unspecified reasons he didn't want to bother Kirby. When he came by my office to give me the check, dated August 1, he had an issue of *Pulpsmith* to show me. It included a reprint of 'The Hounds of Tindalos'. The editor was a fan. Next issue there would be an interview. He was expecting several checks from foreign sales in August. The final day of the month he phoned to request that I hold off a few more days before depositing his check. Again, he promised to get together soon.

Soon turned out to be the last day of September, when I lugged a box of twenty-four copies of *Pulptime* down to Frank's for his signature. After the customary wait, he came out and we walked over to a new place on West 23rd near Seventh he knew of, a cafeteria. But it turned out it had discontinued its cafeteria service – it was now just a bar. We ordered beer and sandwiches. Frank signed all twenty-four copies, laboriously printing his name. He had the usual items to share – somebody's EOD zine with a reprint of 'The Space Eaters', the summer issue of *Pulpsmith* with the interview of him, and a new Berkeley paperback edition of *The Hounds of Tindalos*. Bob had asked him to write another story, had even supplied an outline, but for fifty dollars he wasn't sure it was worth it. "You have to write a novel to make real money. I hope I can come up with a strong one." The following week he'd be meeting Kirby to discuss his novel-in-progress.

On rereading *Pulptime* Frank said he had enjoyed it all the more. "Of course, you got a few things wrong – not that they matter. Having a lively story is the important thing." He then proceeded to enumerate my faults. HPL had three or four ways of speaking, but he would never have used slang at that period, only in his letters. Morton never used slang, and he would never have mentioned sex in conversation as I had him do at one point. The line, 'And when they dragged your weary flesh through Baltimore – did you betray the ticket, Poe?' I had his younger self quote from Hart Crane's 'The Bridge' had a very clear meaning to him – genius abused. (One theory has it that, shortly before his death, Poe fell victim on election day to partisans who got citizens drunk so they could vote several times.) Speaking of politics, Frank admitted he'd been on the left in the past and despaired of Reagan. The current mixing of religion and politics would have been unimaginable in another era. His parents had been Baptists, religious but not overly so. Finally, it was time to get back home to Lyda, who hadn't been feeling well and had been sort of depressed for the past week. "Good luck with your book," he said. "You ought to sell three thousand of them."

At the World Fantasy Convention that fall, held in Ottawa, I did my best to push *Pulptime*, which had a first printing of fifteen hundred copies, both paper and cloth. Friday evening, before the hordes were let in for the traditional author signing, Stephen King himself approached where I was sitting at the tables reserved for us mere mortals, seemingly attracted by the promotional poster an artist friend of mine had created for *Pulptime*. He peered from a distance for a moment or two, then went back to his special table, set aside to accommodate the army of book-laden fans who would soon be descending on him.

After my return to New York, Frank called. "This may sound egotistical," he said, "but I'm curious to know if anyone talked about me at the convention." I replied that I remembered hearing his name in passing, even though I hadn't. To my relief the three-minute warning cut us off before I could elaborate further.

V

The day after Christmas Frank called. From the lack of background noise other than a television it appeared the Longs now had a phone. Frank confirmed this and give me the number. He was curious to hear about the recent group gathering in Marblehead, inspired by Lovecraft's 'The Festival', his Yule yarn celebrating the old Massachusetts seaport. I informed him that Bob was getting married in a few days and would be moving back to the South, where he'd grown up. Frank had a story to pass on to him for *Crypt*. He was sorry to see him go, since Bob had been the driving force behind the local gang.

In the background Lyda shouted something. Frank said he worried about her running up a big phone bill, then put her on the line. Feeling I needed to justify my use of her husband in *Pulptime*, I told her Frank would be getting royalty money since it had just been reprinted. After a minute Frank got back on. He confessed he hadn't done a good job getting out Christmas cards. After New Year's we'd get together.

Later that night, to my surprise, Lyda called. It seemed she hadn't focused on who I was during our earlier chat. "I wanted to tell you how original your book was," she said. "How much better than the usual science fiction-fantasy crap. It's beautifully produced too." From my voice she took me to be in my twenties. I said I was thirty-three but looked younger. She liked the fact that I'd dedicated the book to my grandparents. She spoke of her own family, who had been in the Yiddish theater under the czars. She'd written an account of her grandfather and was planning to do her own life though she was no writer. When she asked if I'd read Dostoevsky's *The Idiot*, I said no. "There's a character in it who's just like Frank – smart, talented, modest, but easily taken advantage of." Then she asked, "Did you know we eloped?" Again I said no. "Frank proposed to me an hour after we met. Twenty-five years we've been married and it's still like the first day!" She closed by promising to have some of us over soon.

Early in the new year I phoned Frank to schedule a get-together. Eager to discuss his autobiography with ST, the editor of Necronomicon Press, he suggested we go out to dinner in the neighborhood. Then Lyda got on. She had in mind making a social occasion of it at their apartment, not going out. When I said a Lovecraft scholar would be along, referring to ST, she said, "I'm not a great fan of Lovecraft's. He stole my thunder by marrying someone like me, a Russian Jew, and Frank had to follow his example!" When Frank got back on, I reassured him Bob was going ahead with the special Long issue of *Crypt*. He'd just written Bob a long letter saying he was ready with a new story.

In the event we did go out, for a 'business' meeting, but not before Frank called to accuse me of misinforming him that Bob had moved to Mississippi. I had in truth told him that Bob was originally from Mississippi and had recently moved to North Carolina. (I could identify with HPL when he complained in his letters about Frank's tendency to mix things up.

"These Yankees think Southern states are all the same" was Bob's comment.) Dinner, at the Chelsea Square, proved an awkward affair, with Frank admitting he didn't really have much to discuss with ST about his autobiography. He brought a couple of items to show us – a Spanish edition of his tales and a book of black-and-white photographs of SF authors. The one of himself was excellent.

At the end of February Lyda called. "I'm still planning to send you my memoir," she said, "but I've been under pressure of a deadline." She was aware of the second printing of *Pulptime*. "You see Frank's name does count for something."

In April Frank called to say he could have his autobiography ready in two weeks if Marc could give him a check for the remaining advance immediately on delivery of the manuscript. "I could be paid better if I did other sorts of writing," he said, "but this is important." I alerted ST, who promised he'd call Marc to let him know. I phoned Frank back to tell him that he should soon be hearing from Marc. Frank asked me about *Pulptime*. He said he continued to plug it to his correspondents. Since things were somewhat confused at his place that evening, we left it that I'd call him the next day at around the same time. Twenty-four hours later Lyda answered the phone after about ten rings and put Frank on. Marc had reached him the previous night and all was well. He thanked me for my efforts.

By the middle of May ST let me know he had Frank's manuscript in hand. The two of them had met for a drink recently at the Chelsea Square, where Frank had griped about Stephen King's good fortune. A week later Marc phoned to ask if I'd like to write a foreword to Frank's memoir. I said I wouldn't have thought one was necessary, but Marc explained that Frank had said little about himself (he mentioned Lyda only once in passing, and not by name). I agreed to do it. After all, he had done me a similar favor.

A few days later, as I was making some notes for the foreword, the man himself called. He was anxious about the status of his autobiography. I told him it had reached Necronomicon Press and was scheduled to come out in July. I declined to mention my own role in the project. Frank was also concerned that the new Arkham House novel with Lovecraft as a character would portray HPL as a racist. *Lovecraft's Book*, by the science fiction author Richard Lupoff, had been out a couple of weeks and was dedicated to him. He hadn't seen a copy yet. (I shortly acquired a copy of *Lovecraft's Book*, whose view of Lovecraft was certainly no more damning than that of de Camp's biography. *Pulptime* had underlined his racist side as well.)

At the end of May I received a photocopy of Frank's *Autobiographical Memoir*, as it was to be called, from Marc, who now suggested I do an 'afterword' instead. Frank had already written an introduction. It was only about fifty pages, much of it handwritten. A superficial glance indicated that it was a lot of hot air, low on substance. A close reading confirmed my initial impression. With few specific anecdotes of interest, it was far worse than *Dreamer on the Nightside*. The style was particularly wordy, the opening sentence epitomizing the whole: 'It is often taken for granted – I've always felt quite unjustifiably – that a fiction writer's characters are thinly disguised aspects of himself wearing multiple-personality type costumes.' The final paragraph of my afterword opened, 'Champion of the florid, extravagant poetry and prose that flourished in the decadent era just before his birth…', an awkward attempt to put the best face on his clumsy prose.

When I met ST a week later to deliver the finished afterword, we agreed that Frank's forte was as a poet or prose-poet. He had never been able to sustain any longer piece, fiction or non-fiction, with any coherence. ST remarked that Frank had received a total of six hundred dollars for the memoir from Necronomicon, a sizeable advance for a small press.

Toward the end of June Lyda phoned, from the intensive care unit of the hospital, she claimed, sounding hale and hearty. She was full of plans for Frank's enemies. First and foremost was Kirby, whom she resented for failing to get any of Frank's stories adapted for the new *Twilight Zone* television series. "Even though Kirby gives Frank a hundred dollars from time to time, I feel he has his worst interests at heart," she said. "Why did Stephen King choose Kirby as his agent? Because King admired Frank so much and Kirby, then a nobody, was Frank's agent." Tom was next on the list, though he hadn't been on the scene for years. She was sure he had moved next door in order to exploit Frank, whom he used to ask to look after his cats when he was away. Furthermore, Tom had spread the rumor that she was manic-depressive. "My 'idiot' would die if he knew I was telling you all this, so mum's the word."

Lyda admitted she was seventy-seven years old, "three times your age." It was their twenty-fifth anniversary, but they hadn't had much of a celebration. "It kills me when Frank has to borrow money from you." She indicated she had a press conference in the works about her book on the Yiddish theater in czarist Russia. She would promote my book as well. "I'd like to meet you," she said. "I'll call again." Which she did a short time later, to suggest I phone them at four the next day so she could invite me to dinner.

At a quarter past three the following day Frank called to tell me not to phone at four. "Lyda and I have had a big fight," he said, "and I fear we're breaking up." He wanted to talk to me, but it would have to wait. That night Lyda called. "We're having guests for dinner tomorrow and you're invited," she said. I had to decline. "Anyway, we need to borrow fifteen dollars – no, better make it twenty-five – to pay for it, so you and Frank have to get together." She had a few choice words on how she was going to get Kirby before abruptly hanging up.

When Frank stopped by my office to give me a check, he seemed in reasonably good spirits. He'd recently heard from Tom, who wasn't happy with his job. "I'd like to do a collection of my short stories, ten old and ten new," he said, "but everyone tells me I have to do a novel first." He was upset by *Lovecraft's Book*, which he felt portrayed HPL inaccurately. Naive fans would get the wrong idea. Why hadn't Arkham House consulted him? "But as I have no wish to offend Lupoff," he said, "there's not much I can do." He appreciated the dedication. When he said he'd heard nothing about his memoir, I told him it would be out soon. "I could've written some more if I'd had another couple of days."

Three days later Lyda called at seven in the morning to invite me to dinner at seven that night. When I arrived at their building, bottle of wine in hand, no one answered the buzzer. Then Frank showed up from the street. "I was expecting you at eight," he said. "In any event, Lyda's asleep and we have nothing to feed you." After some debate whether I should just go home, Frank decided he should wake her. I waited. When he came back he said her first impulse was to see me, then she felt she just couldn't.

Frank walked me to the corner, emphasizing again what a mess it all was and how he might have to leave her. "Maybe next week you can visit," he said, "or at least you and she can talk on the phone." He wasn't keen on their going on TV, which for some reason seemed to be a possibility. "She'll just say I'm the greatest science fiction writer in the world, which won't do me any good."

The following day I spoke with both of them in the morning. We arranged that I would come that night for dinner, with my 'girlfriend' (I wasn't ready to introduce Julie to the Longs as my fiancée).

VI

About a week after that unforgettable night Lyda phoned – to invite us back for dinner that evening. Either she or Frank, it was unclear who, was going into the hospital soon for 'internal bleeding' and she wanted to have a party beforehand. I hemmed and hawed, saying I'd phone later. When we spoke that evening, she said she was exhausted and we'd better call it off. It was she who was going into the hospital the next day. In the meantime she'd arranged with a bookstore in Woodstock, where she once lived, for an autographing party (for *Pulptime*? *Autobiographical Memoir*? both books?).

The following Friday Frank called. He wished to see me in the evening, but since I was leaving that afternoon for New England to attend a local convention, he was willing simply to talk on the phone. Lyda was in the hospital for tests on a growth similar to Reagan's. She had wanted me to visit her, but he would explain how I wasn't available. "Don't take anything she said the other evening seriously," he reiterated. On the other hand, things were now relatively serene in the Long household. He was once again 'wonderful' in Lyda's eyes. He'd recently gotten a check from 'Crawford' for fifteen dollars.

In mid-July Frank called to report he'd received copies of his *Autobiographical Memoir*, which pleased him immensely on rereading. He liked my afterword, except for the last paragraph characterizing him as a champion of florid prose. "I once wrote that way," he admitted, "but not anymore. I'm afraid this comment could wreck my chances to get my novel published. Editors will think I'm old-fashioned." He and Lyda would both like to see a correction made, say, a new paragraph pasted over the old mentioning his Life Achievement Award and First Fandom Hall of Fame Award. I said I'd consult Marc and see what could be done. Frank was surprised when I told him four or five hundred copies had been published. He'd been expecting a figure more like two thousand. Afterwards I regretted not having run the manuscript by Frank before publication, but I was confident Marc could come up with a solution.

When later that day I reached Marc, we agreed to deceive Frank. I would write a new paragraph and he would have it typeset and a patch put over the offending text in a few copies. (To atone further, I would write a review praising the memoir for *Lovecraft Studies*, under a pseudonym.) The following day Lyda called from St. Vincent's Hospital, where she was recuperating. "I'm very European," she said. "I expect flowers." After work I stopped by a florist and ordered the cheapest arrangement they had. The day after that, she phoned to thank me. "How did you know red was my favorite color?" I sent Frank a copy of the new paragraph for his approval.

When Frank next called he wanted to know if I'd heard from Lyda recently. "She's in a down mood again." Everything seemed to be okay, but the doctors were somewhat vague. "I'm to have a long talk with a doctor tomorrow and hopefully get the straight story." As for the substitute paragraph, he mentioned it only briefly before raising a new complaint – a typo on the first page, where the word *mandatory* had been misspelled *manditory*. I told him not to worry about it. "You could write over the wrong letter with a pen and put 'p.e.' in the margin," he suggested. "Maybe there'll be a paperback sale." As usual I wasn't about to disillusion him. Publishers on occasion do provide errata sheets, but no self-respecting press would ever mark a 'printer's error' in a finished book – or as here in a thin stapled booklet, the modest format of all Necronomicon Press publications of that period. In whatever form, the memoir was an extremely unlikely candidate for mass paperback.

At the end of the month Frank called to borrow fifty dollars. Lyda got on the phone to say she was about to take off for China. She invited the whole gang to visit soon. "Just name the day!" I explained I was leaving for Massachusetts shortly. Frank appeared early that afternoon with his check. All his friends were out of town, he didn't want to bother Kirby, so once again he'd come to me for help. "This is the very last time," he vowed. He asked me to tell Marc to call him to discuss the memoir. He was less troubled by my closing paragraph (in fact he appreciated it all the more on rereading) than by the 'mandatory' typo. He confessed he was growing a full beard, was in his sixth day, hence his seedy appearance.

Before leaving Frank gave me a pair of envelopes from Lyda. The larger one included, among other odd items, a sheet of parchment-like floral stationery, evidently the paper used to announce their wedding (on one side she'd written 'Lyda Arco Frank Belknap Long became one August 13, 1960'). The other, a perfumed pink envelope, contained a short letter, which read in part: 'Have just again reread the afterword – even shed a tear. My Frankele so truthfully presented – thank you!' She closed, 'Best to Janet. Lydasha.' An hour later Lyda phoned. "Frank's going to be on ABC's *Good Morning America* in two weeks," she crowed. She'd been in touch with Joe Franklin. "One good turn deserves another!"

While on vacation I sent Frank a postcard with the news of my engagement. Soon after returning to New York I got a call from Lyda. Joe Franklin was coming by the next morning to pick up copies of both *Pulptime* and Frank's memoir. "Frank doesn't want to go on the show," she said. "I think you should fill in."

A week later, while I was out of the office, Lyda came by to pick up copies of *Pulptime* and *Autobiographical Memoir* for delivery to Joe Franklin. At the reception desk she'd left two packages. One contained a peasant shirt for 'Jennie', the other an assortment of photocopied newspaper clippings and collage-like notes all to do with herself. The next day she called to make sure I'd gotten everything. "Joe Franklin likes to help young writers and artists," she said. "His son is a big fan of Frank's." She promised to have me scheduled as a guest on the show by the following week.

I showed Julie the peasant shirt. It was a size fit for a child and scarcely her style. Julie wrote Lyda a gracious thank you note. A few days later Lyda called to tell me she'd set a date with Joe Franklin. She asked me to return her 'autobiography', the materials she'd left off the other day. "Please thank Jennie for her note," she added.

Further calls from Lyda finally fixed a date with Franklin in early September, at his studio in Times Square. She wasn't sure if she would make it, but if she did we could all meet afterwards at the Algonquin. At one point Frank got on the line to bitch about the 'mandatory' typo. "I'd like it corrected in time for the World Fantasy Convention." I mailed Lyda's 'autobiography' back to her.

At the appointed hour I showed up at the WOR studio just as one taping session of *The Joe Franklin Show* was ending and another beginning. There was no sign of Lyda, who had telephoned the night before to assure me she'd be there at five. I took a seat in the waiting area, where I signed a disclaimer and nervously waited my turn. I had slept badly. From talking to friends I was aware that just about anybody who wanted to could and did appear on *Joe Franklin*, the more off-beat or even crazy the better. I was unlikely to sell many extra copies of my book as a result. Nonetheless, the opportunity to be on television, any television, was one I felt I shouldn't pass up.

Suddenly the taping was over. I was not going to get on, not that day at any rate. Someone on the staff called my name. I had a visitor. It was Frank. After telling me Lyda was in terrible shape and couldn't make it, he led me over to the stage to introduce me to Joe Franklin. Evidently Lyda had failed to confirm my appearance earlier in the day as she was supposed to, but Franklin was happy to reschedule me for the following week. He suggested I bring a couple of copies of my book, plus whatever promotional materials I had. He didn't know anything really about science fiction, he admitted, but his son was a fan of Frank's. "One of the greats," he said, "one of the greats." Maybe Frank could take a bow, assuming he'd be there too. Frank said he and Lyda had been on the show eight years earlier.

The two of us left together. On the walk to the subway Frank went on about how pleased he was with my afterword, except for the last paragraph. For what seemed like the thousandth time I heard how his style was in fact quite modern, how editors might be misled by my statement, how– I welcomed the din of the 42nd Street station.

That night Julie told me Lyda had called her at home in Brooklyn. She'd put her return address on the envelope of her thank you note, allowing Lyda to get her number from information. Lyda had repeated the whole rambling story of her and Frank. Now she wanted to have lunch, just the two of them. Julie dreaded the prospect.

On the next attempt I appeared on *Joe Franklin* without a hitch, better prepared and more relaxed than I'm sure I would have been had the previous try not ended in anticlimax. While reluctant to part with it, I gave Franklin the copy of *Autobiographical Memoir* Marc had sent me with the new last paragraph. It was for his son. (Marc had also sent Frank the 'corrected' text, the only other copy.) Lyda and Frank didn't show. When I talked with them that evening, I learned they had arrived two hours late. "Nevermind," said Lyda. "We got double exposure – even better than if we'd been on the same program." Frank had spoken on camera for a few minutes, and signed his memoir for Franklin's son.

A few days later Lyda called. She asked me to send her a New Year's card, that is, a Jewish New Year's card. "All my friends are dead or out of the country," she said. She reiterated how much she liked Julie (finally she had the name right). They were planning a twenty-fifth wedding anniversary party in October. She confessed that when she got high she phoned all her friends.

A few days after that she called again. "Where's my New Year's card?" she asked. (Lyda rarely bothered to say hello or identify herself at the start of a phone conversation.) I said I'd only mailed it that morning. She and Frank had been strolling in the Village earlier. "He pins up his trousers rather than go to a tailor," she said. "What can you expect of a man who didn't get married until his late fifties? His full beard is very becoming. He's quite vain."

The next night Julie and I stayed up late to watch my TV debut. "*Pulptime*, it's sure to be a good time," quipped Franklin as he introduced me. Despite a shiny forehead and a certain nervousness evident at the start, I thought I did okay. In context I saw that I had received, understandably enough, much less air time than the guests paired with me, Kit McClure and another member of her all-girl swing band. Afterwards – it was a quarter of two in the morning – Lyda called to congratulate me on my sensational performance.

The next night I stayed up even later, to catch Frank's performance, which came at the end of the show, right after a rap group did their thing. Frank was utterly unselfconscious. "Just in the last four or five months – no, no, I mean ten or fifteen years – there's been a tremendous upsurge of interest in science fiction and supernatural horror," he began. Joe Franklin described the show as a kind of time capsule. When he asked what Frank thought people would make of it in ten thousand years, Frank expressed his usual pessimism about the future of mankind. As the credits rolled, Franklin pressed him about his most important early literary influence – "It was HP Lovecraft, right?" In a soft but firm voice Frank replied no, it was primarily sea and adventure stories. As deadpan comedy it was brilliant.

VII

A day or two later Lyda phoned. "Guess what?" she said. "When Frank went into the grocery store and the liquor store today, everyone recognized him! Now we don't have to worry about our grocery bills!" Frank had been reluctant to go on TV, she conceded, but it had all worked out happily.

At the end of September Frank came by to borrow thirty dollars. He looked better dressed than usual, may even have been wearing new clothes. His mood was cheerful. He wanted to get together soon. "I have a lot to talk with you about." He had a present from Lyda, this time for both me and Julie, a collection of prose-poems printed in brown ink by a woman named Nina Balaban. Later I looked at this little self-published booklet carefully. Entitled *In Earth's Bondage* and published by 'Lydacia Press' in 1966, it contained sixteen rather mystical prose-poems in Russian with English translations on facing pages. It opened with a two-page 'In Appreciation' by Frank that impressed me as being as fine as his best poetry. Lyda had inscribed it to us with the message 'Eternal Bliss!' She had signed it from Lydasha, Frankele, and Shim Sham (their dog), and dated it August 13, 1985.

A couple of weeks later Frank phoned. He had several things on his mind, foremost the essay on himself in the new Scribner's *Supernatural Fiction Writers* encyclopedia. Written by Les Daniels, a horror writer and pulp culture historian, it was I saw – when I read it later that fall – a sympathetic and intelligent critical appraisal of which Frank had every reason to be proud. As usual he was under a lot of pressure, but he promised to call again in a few days.

More than a week later we spoke. Frank more or less repeated what he told me our last conversation, except this time he complained about editors who put too many semi-colons in his work. In particular Joshi, the editor of his memoir, had been guilty of this sin. "Semi-colons are old-fashioned or else academic," he said. "I don't use them these days."

We were finally able to arrange a get-together for a Saturday afternoon in mid-November. ST and I met him at his door and we walked over to the Chelsea Square. We stopped at a drugstore so Frank could pick up a prescription for Lyda, who he said hadn't been well lately. At the restaurant Frank had a briefcase full of items to show us, including a copy of the favorable piece from the Scribner's volume. ST gave him a copy of a booklet put out in England devoted to the Welsh fantasist Arthur Machen – which included Frank's sonnet 'On Reading Arthur Machen'. Frank was both surprised and pleased. According to ST, his contact in England had gotten Frank's permission to reprint the poem, but Frank had no recollection of this transaction. (HPL had cited it in full in his survey *Supernatural Horror in Literature*, probably without asking Frank either.)

From his briefcase Frank produced one unexpected item – a letter from an official committee planning to celebrate the Statue of Liberty's centennial in '87. He was going to meet with some people from this group on Tuesday. He seemed to think somebody at my office would know whether they were legitimate or not. "I hope they're important enough to want to pay a lot of money for this signed book I have." Frank's grandfather, Charles O Long, had been the contractor who built the pedestal for the Statue of Liberty and later served as its first superintendent. Frank told me once that his family had possessed the American flag used in the dedication ceremony, so it was entirely possible he had a valuable relic or two preserved from that era. I said I'd see what I could do.

Another potential big money-maker was his uncompleted novel. "Kirby told me he could get me a two-hundred-thousand-dollar advance on a really strong one." He confessed he had to keep working to pay for the basics of life. "At my age I'd gladly give up writing if I had enough to live on." Apropos of Lovecraft, he mentioned that once, provoked by a museum Civil War exhibit, Howard had called General Sherman a barbarian.

A few days later Frank phoned to report that he'd had a good meeting with the Statue of Liberty people, at the Chelsea Square. He would have to loan them his souvenir book, though. If he wanted to get any money for it, he'd have to sell it elsewhere. I said nobody at my office knew the organization. Frank meant to write Marc to thank him for correcting the last paragraph of my afterword, and to ask for more copies of the memoir. "I'm curious to know how it sold at the World Fantasy Convention. Do you know?" Since I hadn't attended that year, I couldn't enlighten him.

The last day of December Lyda phoned to wish me Happy New Year. She'd been calling up all her friends by way of celebration. When she offered to be my agent, I said I'd be honored but had done no work in which an agent would be interested. Full of good cheer, she announced that she was going to open a Russian restaurant in 1986. "The Russian Tea Room's a fake!" She claimed she had a backer with money. It would be called 'Lydasha's'. In the new year she expected to get to Boston, where she hoped to meet my grandparents. When I explained my grandparents lived in California, she said she meant my parents. She was planning to agent a Ray Bradbury play in Boston. I wished her and Frank a Happy New Year from Julie and myself.

In January I received a series of calls, some of them no more than a few seconds long, from Lyda. Frank's *Dreamer* was a bad book because he was so harassed when he wrote it. She was plotting her revenge on Kirby for the World Fantasy Convention that fall. President Reagan was sending her to Russia as a cultural envoy. Frank, incidentally, was deathly afraid of the Soviets. She needed help with the materials she'd been collecting for her various 'books'. Would one of my sisters be interested in doing the necessary errands? "Money's no object!" (I'd revealed that I had two younger sisters, both living in New York.) Later she called back to say she'd found a student at the seminary across the street to take care of her work. My sisters were spared, but not my fiancée, who objected to Lyda's phoning so early in the morning.

One morning Lyda called three times in a row. "I'd like you to order a hundred copies of Frank's memoir for me," she said. "I'm planning a big party." I promised to get in touch with Marc. "Of course, I want the corrected version." She also asked me to order a hundred copies of *Pulptime* for placement in various stores in Chelsea, "run by those homo sapiens" (homosexuals?). In the neighborhood everyone knew and loved Frank. I said I'd send her some flyers with ordering information to distribute. Later I wrote Marc warning him Lyda might be placing a large order for Frank's memoir.

The next day I sent Lyda some flyers for *Pulptime*, along with a note requesting that she not call me before noon on the weekends. A few days later she phoned, full of apologies for having called too early. I heard how in October they'd traveled by bus to Texas to attend the World Fantasy Convention, after cashing in the plane tickets the organizers had sent Frank. He had received the Life Achievement Award.

Finally, one night Frank called – from the street, as in the old days. He didn't want Lyda to know he was phoning me. He was concerned about her ordering hundreds of copies of our books. I said I'd alerted Marc to the situation. Again Frank said he was going to write Marc soon to thank him for the splendid job he'd done on the memoir. He wanted to get together with me for a long talk.

In February Lyda called with ideas of bargain Valentine's Day presents for me to give Julie. "I'm very pleased with Frank's memoir, the look of it and all," she said, "but is there any chance of doing it in hardcover?" Not unless he rewrote and expanded it, I answered. She had read the interview with Stephen King in the current *Interview*. "I assume he uses four-letter words because that's the custom these days." (In general Lyda regarded King favorably, since he once serenaded her at a convention with his guitar.)

Lyda phoned the day after Valentine's. "Frank never gets me a present," she said. "He scrambles around at the last minute. So I called up my favorite stationery store and ordered them to send me their best card signed 'Frankele'." They'd had their kitchen redone. Frank apparently wanted to save a cockroach to mount. In his youth he used to collect insects as a hobby. She confessed their phone bill for the past month had been $350. She also said she was drunk – on vodka. This led to a discussion of the likes of Yevteshenko and Pasternak, the last whom she claimed to have known or at least met. Yevteshenko's new movie had no plot, but was excellent on showing the Russian character. On the other hand, the recent *Peter the Great* on TV was garbage.

In March both Lyda and Frank phoned one night after eleven. Lyda ranted about Kirby, while Frank said he'd like to have lunch soon with me and Joshi. He was worried about the forthcoming special Long issue of *Crypt*. "People will get the impression that I haven't changed my style any," he said, "when in fact I'm now writing in a very different fashion." Lyda said we could all have lunch in their new kitchen.

When ST and I showed up a few days later, Frank came to the door and informed us Lyda wasn't well, the plumbers had been in, the place was a mess – he'd meet us at the Chelsea Square in ten minutes. ST and I had started our lunch by the time he joined us. Frank ordered soup and a vodka on the rocks, straight up. When the drink came he complained it was too strong.

Frank first groused about Bob's decision to drop one of the stories he'd written for the Long issue of *Crypt*, relegating it to a new magazine devoted to spaceship fiction or some such that he feared wouldn't be as well known as *Crypt*. "I wanted to write Bob a three-page letter explaining what a mistake that would be," he said, "but I just don't have the time." He lamented the passing of a number of his friends and associates, including Wilfred Talman, who had been a later recruit to the Kalems. Lester Del Rey still bore him a grudge since a long ago feud divided the science fiction writers of the time. He was sure Del Rey had avoided the World Fantasy Convention because of his receipt of the Life Achievement Award.

Frank Herbert had taken the worm image for *Dune* from a short story of his in *Weird Tales*, he asserted, while Stephen King had gotten the idea for 'the shining' from a story of his about a boy drifting down the Mississippi on a raft. He didn't resent either author. In fact, he was grateful, presumably for the satisfaction of having inspired them. Frank admitted he'd left out the whole middle part of his memoir – an account of his relationships with writers and editors for the past several decades. ST and I suggested the possibility of his writing an article to supplement the memoir, without the burden of a deadline. Marc could maybe pay him a hundred dollars.

Thanks to the vodka, which had become more and more drinkable as the ice melted, Frank was more candid on personal matters than usual. "Loveman was never an active homosexual," he said. "He would never have had sex with Hart Crane, his boyhood friend. Crane, on the other hand, was always picking up sailors." (To that degree my cameo of Crane in *Pulptime* was accurate, I noted smugly.) "Howard and the rest knew of it, but that didn't affect their friendship with Crane." HPL and James Morton, another Kalem, had had very different tastes and views, yet were great pals. When I mentioned that Jill, an EOD member and fan of his, had recently divorced and remarried, he said, "It always amazes me how quickly people marry and divorce these days." Finally, Frank asked ST for the address of Les Daniels, whom he wished to write to thank for his essay.

VIII

In May I tried to phone Frank, to arrange a get-together with Jill and her new husband Richard, but discovered their number had been disconnected. In early June a call from Lyda confirmed this was the case. "We want to give you a wedding present," she said. "An oak side-table." I wrote Frank and Lyda a card thanking them for their kind offer and saying we hoped to see them after our wedding, scheduled for Saturday the 14th. (Since we were to leave the following day for two weeks in Sicily, with any luck it would be well into the summer before we saw the Longs again.)

We saw them the Tuesday before the wedding. Despite all Julie and I still had to do to get ready for the big event, we accepted their invitation – for dinner on their roof, which proved a far more appealing locale, with its open views, than their hall. This time we came better prepared, bringing a bottle of champagne and plastic champagne glasses. The Longs provided chairs. The weather was sunny and clear. Frank went out to shop, returning with nuts and a selection of deli salads. He forgot to buy orange juice for the vodka, but at least there were enough glasses to go around. They both stayed sober. Lyda held forth but said nothing overly embarrassing. Frank had written a new story, for an anthology edited by Dennis Etchison, which needed typed. Evidently he no longer had a working typewriter. Maybe Joshi could do it. They presented us with their wedding gift – a collapsible TV tray, on wheels no less. Very practical. While they did ask why we'd chosen Sicily for our honeymoon, they didn't otherwise show much interest in our lives. We left before it got dark. I sent them a postcard from Sicily.

Late in July the Longs called. They needed twenty or twenty-five bucks. No, we weren't free to join them for dinner tomorrow, but I said when I stopped by we'd try to arrange something. In February I'd joined ST on the staff of a reference book publisher in the Village. It was easy to get to their place on my lunch hour. When I arrived Lyda was in her wheelchair on the sidewalk in front of 421, their dog beside her. She didn't recognize me at first. "So young," she muttered. Frank appeared. "Better make it thirty," he said as I reached for my wallet. We set Friday evening for dinner, to include ST. I later sent them a card telling them also to expect Jill and her husband. Everyone would bring something to eat or drink. Julie and I agreed there was strength in numbers.

After work ST and I walked over to the Longs', where again we found Lyda sitting out front. We took a seat on a neighboring stoop while we waited for Frank, who was buying groceries. Lyda worried about him. He'd been mugged three times over the years. "Once, in the hallway outside the apartment, thieves stripped him of his pants," she said. "They thought the truss he was wearing for his hernia was a money belt." When, questioned about himself, ST replied "What's there to say?," she continued with her monologue.

We were about to leave a note at the entrance saying we'd gone to the roof when Frank toddled into view. He led us to the roof while Lyda stayed below. For a summer evening in New York it wasn't too humid. Frank disappeared, but it wasn't long before he returned with Julie, Jill and Richard. We helped Lyda up the final flight of stairs to the roof. Our hosts provided the usual selection of deli treats, including whole scallions. As the first item of business, Julie, Jill and Richard excused themselves to go use the Longs' bathroom. They took a key downstairs. I was dying to know what they'd discovered in the inner sanctum, but had to be patient until the party was over. Before we could pour the wine, Frank had to return to the apartment to get a corkscrew. (So they did have one after all.)

Lyda didn't zero in on Julie the way she had in the past, though at one point she declared, "You don't look as *zaftig* as I remember." It was not the sort of personal remark Julie appreciated. The rest of us chuckled nervously. Lyda did virtually all the talking until Frank, apropos of nothing, launched into a sententious speech about the greatest minds being those who were the greatest innovators. By this standard Shakespeare didn't make the list, but one of the early Greek philosophers did (I forget which). A sudden cloudburst put an end to our picnic. We hastened inside and regrouped in the apartment below.

At last my curiosity was satisfied to learn what lay beyond the first ten feet of the hall. First came a closed door on the left, to the bedroom, then another door, to the bathroom. The hall widened into an alcove and at the end was a tiny kitchen, which we shunned. To the right was a sunken living room. It was dark but there was enough light from the hall to tell it was filled with debris, while festoons of paint hung from the ceiling. "The man on the floor above has a clubfoot," said Lyda, as if that explained the ceiling problem. (I was reminded that earlier she'd told ST and me that Frank had recently trod by accident on their marriage certificate – I could now see why that was easy to do.) The bathroom was the neatest room in the place, decorated with posters that Lyda said she changed every week. "Some of them anyway," she added.

"I want to get out of here," Julie hissed to me. We didn't linger.

Jill and Richard gave us a ride in their car to the subway. "An interesting evening," said Richard. Indeed, visiting the Longs' was definitely a novelty, but as Julie noted the experience soon began to wear thin. Jill said she thought at first there were bats hanging from the living room ceiling. Julie said the bedroom was as foul as the living room. She had no idea where they slept. We speculated that the bathtub was Lyda's bed.

More than a week later I came home to find a message from Frank on our answering machine. He complained that a lot of valuable stuff was lost in the aftermath of the party, including Lyda's pipe. He seemed to want some sort of restitution but hesitated to ask for it outright.

In September I received the contract for my next major book project – a critical study of Lovecraft for Twayne's US Authors Series. Various others had been under contract, but since the publisher paid only a modest royalty and no advance I gathered my predecessors had lacked motivation. Writing a scholarly survey of HPL's fiction soon became a higher priority than looking after his aging best friend. Julie and I went to Providence for the World Fantasy Convention, where Paul Ganley gave me a copy of Frank's Arkham House poetry collection, *In Mayan Splendor*, for Frank's signature. The Longs did not go, rumor having it that Lyda was sick. Afterwards I wrote Frank a postcard saying he was missed.

The third week of December Frank called. He was under the usual terrible pressures but there was one bright spot – he'd received a contract for his novel. Kirby had clearly come through on his behalf, though I wouldn't have been surprised to learn that the editor had done it as an act of charity. I congratulated him, promising we'd get together after Christmas.

In the new year we were blessed to hear nothing from the Longs for months. Finally I felt it was time to check up on them. In April, a few days before leaving New York on a six-week leave of absence to work full-time on my Twayne study, I stopped by their building and pushed the buzzer for 1-A. Frank came to the door then went back inside to get his hat. Since it was a warm day he took off his hat, along with the lightweight blue blazer he was wearing. As it happened, I was wearing an almost identical blue blazer. At some point, while we stood chatting on the sidewalk, I may have removed my blazer too and hung it over my arm.

The advance for the novel was allowing them to live more comfortably of late, he indicated, though "another ten or fifteen hundred dollars would be a big help." Lyda was apparently in need of a cataract operation. He was hoping for a television or even a movie sale. He was annoyed that he'd heard nothing from Marc since his memoir came out. He'd be willing to write up the part he left out – that is, an account of HPL's Brooklyn days. (Evidently he'd forgotten that he'd theoretically covered that subject in *Dreamer*.)

Frank regretted not having been in touch recently. "I was going to write you a card asking the best times to reach you," he said. About forty unanswered fan letters had piled up. When he said he wished to have lunch with me and ST soon, I explained I wasn't going to be around for the next six weeks. "I know Joshi doesn't think much of my *Dreamer*, but I've gotten many favorable responses to it," he said. "Including a couple from film makers in Providence."

Frank was keen to hear what went on at the World Fantasy Convention, as well as at the recent fiftieth-anniversary observance in Providence of HPL's death. Due to Lyda's ill health he'd been unable to attend these events, even with the promise of all expenses paid. Two recent tributes especially pleased him – an appreciation in the Long issue of *Crypt*, by Ben Indick, and inclusion in the *Penguin Encyclopedia of Horror and the Supernatural*. It was particularly gratifying that he'd received a longer entry than Jack London, one of his boyhood idols. (When I later compared them, I saw that he'd gotten fifty lines to his boyhood idol's forty-nine. Ben had written the one on him, Ted the one on London.) He criticized the author of the London entry for not mentioning *The Sea Wolf*, though he also referred to it as *The Sea Rover*. "Probably never even read it," he muttered. I told him of my contract with Twayne. It astounded him that I'd been given no advance for it. "No wonder they can't get anybody," he said. He signed Paul's copy of *In Mayan Splendor* while I held his hat. As I left he said, "Please send my greetings to your wife."

The next day Frank left a message on our machine accusing me of walking off with his jacket. That he might have misplaced it in the jungle of their apartment didn't seem to have occurred to him. "I hope you and Joshi can join me for lunch either Thursday or Friday," he added. I relayed this invitation to ST, who promised to get in touch with Frank somehow. He would run the idea of Frank's doing another memoir past Marc. The day before Julie and I left for Massachusetts I wrote Frank a card saying I was sorry I wouldn't be able to see him for lunch.

IX

A gain all was quiet on the Long front for months. (When after my return to the city I'd asked ST if he'd seen Frank in my absence, he said he hadn't because he never heard from Frank.) Then Lyda called the first week of October. She'd just gotten out of the hospital. "Have you received the jacket of my forthcoming book?" she asked. I gathered she meant her history of the Yiddish theater in Russia. I hadn't. She was hoping to make a lot of money for Frank, "the idiot." She was planning a twenty-seventh anniversary party. "I've invited King and Fritz Leiber. I'll keep you posted." Minutes later she phoned again. "I'm hoping to get Frank to a doctor tomorrow," she said. "He has four hernias but refuses to do anything about them." Claiming she was feeling tired, she hung up. Apparently their phone had been reconnected.

The day before Halloween I ran into Lyda sitting in her wheelchair in front of B Altman's, the department store then at Madison and 34th. She was wearing a seasonal orange and black coat. She recognized me, but I had to tell her my name. "Are you wearing a wig?" she asked. "You don't look like you." Maybe I was having a bad hair day. "Frank calls you a pig because you haven't been in touch," she continued in a nastier tone. I protested that I'd made the effort but Frank hadn't responded. As she wheeled off down the sidewalk, I called after her to let me know their new phone number. This chance meeting didn't make me feel good.

Happily, that evening Lyda left a friendly message on our machine with their new number. Another message a couple of days later said Frank was very sick. She was taking him away for a week to get him out of Kirby's clutches. I decided I ought to try to arrange a lunch with Frank soon. But I was busy working on my critical study and I didn't feel like it. From New Mexico, where Julie and I spent Thanksgiving with her uncle and aunt, I mailed Frank a postcard. In mid-December I sent a Christmas card. When we returned from visiting our families in Massachusetts after Christmas, we found Lyda had left a brief acknowledging message.

We heard nothing more until the end of February, when Lyda phoned. "Guess what?" she said. "I'm going to Israel next week. My book's selling well." She put Frank on. As usual he'd been under quite a lot of pressure, trying to finish up his novel. When I told him I'd been working hard on my critical study, he asked to see the manuscript. "Joshi had quite a few errors in his book," he said, referring to a Lovecraft guide ST had done for a specialty press. "I want to make sure you don't make mistakes." Since Lyda was jabbering in the background, he couldn't talk long. In fact she was trying to get him to tell me it was her birthday that day, I could hear. I promised we'd meet soon for lunch. A short time later Lyda phoned again – to tell me it was her eightieth birthday but mainly to berate me for not inviting them over. I said we were having our kitchen redone. "That's no excuse," she said, "when we've had you here so often." I confessed I'd been neglectful. "Frank is very fond of you," she said. "You should have him over, feed him, talk to him."

About two weeks later, shortly after speaking to Lyda from a pay phone on 21st Street, I ran into Frank. He'd been out doing errands. Again he asked to check my Twayne book for errors. "Joshi doesn't always get it right," he said. I waited in the hallway outside the apartment while he went inside. The place was being repainted. A few minutes later he called me in to see Lyda, who was making collages in her bathtub. She was lucid and pleasant enough, though she did harp on the ignorance of 'Lousecraftians'. Frank showed me a French translation of *Dreamer*, which was beautifully produced, with a photograph section at the back. Evidently he had a new French translation of his fiction, but he couldn't find it. I'd have to come back another time. As for his financial situation, "I'm afraid I may have to beg soon on the street with a sign around my neck," he said. "Or maybe Kirby will work some sort of deal that will get me half a million dollars." Then he started to harangue me for having called him a florid writer. "Yes," he admitted, "I did go through a 'yellow nineties' period once but that was long ago. Others have written pointing out how clear my prose is." And so on. I departed with promises of having a proper get-together soon.

In mid-April Lyda phoned about dinner plans. Since we were still reluctant to entertain the Longs at our apartment, we compromised by offering to take them out to dinner in honor of Frank's birthday. The upshot was that Julie and I showed up the evening of the 27th with tulips and cheap champagne for a surprise party chez Long. We were met at the door by an older black gentleman, whom Lyda introduced as an actor named Giles. Years before Giles had performed in a production of *The Cherry Orchard* that Lyda had staged in their living room – which, in contrast to our first visit, was now open to guests. It had been painted and the clutter seemed somewhat organized.

On a shawl-covered trunk Lyda had set out paper plates suitable for a child's birthday and plastic glasses. When Julie suggested we put the champagne on ice, Lyda said they had no refrigerator. I poured a glass of cranberry juice and vodka for each of us. Frank, who'd been out buying orange juice, arrived after a few minutes. Since he'd had a fall earlier in the day and had trouble getting up (Giles had had to help him), he was in no mood for a surprise party, though he seemed pleased enough to see us.

Lyda and Julie sat on the single bed, covered by a thin Indian blanket, that occupied the near corner of the living room. Giles took a seat on the bench in front of the upright piano next to the bed. After opening and pouring the champagne, I joined Frank on the couch at the far end of the room, under the window. Or rather I should say I variously stood and squatted near him, since the junk on the couch allowed room for only one person to sit. Giles showed us some snapshots he'd taken of Lyda holding court in her tub. He had his camera with him and took pictures. Lyda exhibited her latest collage, which included the illustration from the back of *Pulptime* showing Long, Lovecraft, and Holmes. One poignant relic was a fragmentary black-and-white photograph of Frank's father. The face, what was left of it, strongly resembled that of the son.

Frank and I ended up holding our own conversation. He lamented how he couldn't answer any of his fan mail or autograph books people sent him, how he had yet to finish his novel, how he was the last of the Lovecraft circle, how his fame hadn't brought him any money. Then he started talking about his *Autobiographical Memoir*. "*Biographical Memoir* it's called," he said. "Only seven dollars. You should buy a copy." Then he remembered – and took me to task for calling his style old-fashioned.

For dinner we ordered from the Chelsea Square, our treat – mousaka for Julie and me, chicken à la king for Lyda. Unfortunately, Giles left before the meal was delivered, pleading other engagements. Frank shuffled into the kitchen to heat up some Chinese food someone had given them that morning. He complained it was too spicy. Frank cooked on a hot plate, not liking to use the stove. I peeked in the kitchen – litter covered the floor, cockroaches the walls. There was indeed no refrigerator.

During dinner Lyda droned on dropping names. Julie ceased to show the animated interest she'd displayed earlier. It was time to go. As we headed for the door, Frank asked, "Have you heard from Tom?" No, not in a few years, I told him. Frank looked cheerful as he waved us out. On the street Julie reported that at one point during cocktails she'd brushed a cockroach off her eyebrow.

A few weeks later Lyda called, all excited by the recent closing of the musical *Carrie*, based on the Stephen King novel, after opening night. Frank got on briefly to thank us for attending his surprise birthday – and to apologize for not having been in a good mood at the time. Lyda phoned again the next night. Encouraged by Gorbachev's reforms, she was hopeful she could get her history of the Yiddish theater published in Russia. "Now that Heinlein's gone Frank's the only one left," she said, speaking of the late science fiction author. "He will get his due." In her next call, a week later, she read a letter to Frank from Charles Grant, head of the Horror Writers of America. Frank was to receive a special award at their upcoming annual meeting in New York. Included was free accommodations at the Warwick Hotel. "Frank is finally getting his due!" she crowed. The only ominous note was that he'd been falling down a lot lately.

In early June I phoned Frank to invite him to lunch. He was under great pressure, Lyda was depressed. "I can't get over all the terrible things going on in the city," he said. "Eighteen eighty-four is near!" (Presumably he was referring to Orwell's *Nineteen Eighty-four*.) With the Reagan-Gorbachev summit in progress, he had time only to read the newspaper headlines. The next day, on Lyda's advice, I arrived at the apartment a half hour later than planned. I still had to wait fifteen minutes, and even then Frank had to go back inside to get his hat and to exchange Lyda's cane for his own sturdier model, which he couldn't find at first.

At the Chelsea Square Frank ordered a bowl of pea soup and a rum collins. He especially recommended the rum collins. This time he had fewer complaints than usual, though they'd had a wild three days staying with friends of Lyda's in Brooklyn over the Memorial Day weekend. I told him about one fan-scholar's recent discovery that Lovecraft's paternal grandparents were buried in Woodlawn Cemetery in the Bronx. Frank suspected HPL was unaware of this fact when he was living in New York. "My family has a plot in Woodlawn," he added. "That's where I'll be buried."

When I asked if Lovecraft had ever gone swimming in the ocean, Frank responded with the familiar story of how his friend had taken his one and only airplane ride in a seaplane off Onset, on Cape Cod. "The memory of Howard being carried by two men through the surf is still clear as day to me," he said. "I was too scared to go." He knew Joshi didn't believe his accounts of Lovecraft were all that reliable.

Frank spoke of his *Mayflower* ancestor, Edward Doty, who'd been the first English servant in America. "The Pilgrims were religious fanatics," he said. "The evangelicals of their day." When I asked if he'd had any uncles or aunts, he said he had uncles on his father's side. A 'niece', that is, a granddaughter of one of these uncles, lived in Florida, but he hadn't been in touch with her in a few years. He mentioned his connection to Lord Mansfield. (All the aristocratic ancestors appeared to be on his mother's side.) He grumbled a bit about the whole Statue of Liberty business falling through, though he did identify his grandparents in an old photograph taken at the site, presumably provided by one of the committee members who met with him.

Of the assorted items Frank had brought the most interesting was a request from the French publishers of *Dreamer* for sample letters or manuscript material to include in their edition. "I regret not even having replied," he said, "but I couldn't have honored the request anyway." Another item he had to show me was the jacket from *Lovecraft's Book*. "Howard hated Vereick," he said, speaking of the Fascist propagandist with whom HPL collaborates in the novel. And he had a photocopy of his entry from the *Penguin Encyclopedia*. "More space than Jack London," he murmured. I promised to let him review the manuscript of my Twayne study, then nearly finished.

"Bob has accepted a number of my recent stories," he said. "He even sent me an extra fifty dollars. It was supposedly anonymous but I knew who it was." Frank could use more friends like Bob, I thought. "I'd like to see a new story collection of mine published, with ten or fifteen of the old and ten or fifteen of the new," Frank continued. "But it would have to be coordinated with the new novel." He hadn't been able to get ahold of Kirby of late, and was worried about the status of his novel. Since he hadn't heard from Marc in several years, he assumed the memoir had not been a big hit. While I didn't say so, I knew through ST that Marc was in no mood to issue any sort of sequel given his losses on *Autobiographical Memoir*.

X

In mid-summer Lyda phoned – to say they were nearly raped and murdered by intruders Frank had accidentally buzzed in. They'd pretended to be painters come to measure the living room. "The next time you go to Massachusetts you must bring me along," she said, prompted perhaps by the postcard I'd recently sent from my parents'. "I'm planning a big gala for our anniversary this year," she added.

About a week later she left a message on our machine. "Pick up the July issue of *Interview*," she said. "I'm in it." When I called back, Lyda said, "I can't talk. Robbers have broken in the building and the police are chasing them now." The following day Lyda phoned with a more coherent account. Frank had let into the apartment two men claiming to be painters, who then asked for change for fifty dollars. "Since they appeared to be Greek I told them I knew Melina Mercouri," she said, "and sang them a Greek song. Mind you I was naked in the bathtub at the time." All the while Frank had screamed at them to go. Eventually they did leave, without getting any money, but not before they first looked in Frank's bedroom and opened a purse of hers. "We called the police and are only now getting over the excitement." She was going to write Stephen King to ask for his financial help. I gathered she had yet to be interviewed for *Interview*.

Julie answered Lyda's next call. They were having a TV crew in to film their anniversary party. In the meantime they were getting a refrigerator. A couple of days later Lyda phoned and again spoke to Julie. She wanted us to come for dinner that night but we had other plans. Julie despaired that she was falling into this old woman's grasp. The next day I called Lyda hoping to escape another outing to the Longs, but in the end I agreed we'd come by that evening, possibly with another couple, who lived in Brooklyn.

Efforts to persuade our friends to accompany us were to no avail. They'd heard too much about the Longs to be enticed. When we arrived, Frank and Lyda said they were glad we'd come alone. Julie gave Lyda flowers and some seashells she'd collected at the beach in Massachusetts, while I presented Frank with a copy of the complete manuscript of my book. They offered the usual spread – vodka and orange juice and a selection of deli salads. While Lyda talked at Julie, I discussed Lovecraftian matters with Frank. I said Bob was considering writing a critical study of his work for the same company that had published ST's Lovecraft guide. Frank showed me the prize he'd received from the Horror Writers of America in June. It was a weighty ceramic trophy in the form of a 'haunted house', with his name inscribed inside the little front door.

Eventually Lyda began to rant. One senior figure in the field had driven his wife to suicide or was otherwise responsible for her death. "Being gay, he only liked her for display," she asserted. When she spoke highly of another individual Frank objected, and they were soon engaged in a shouting match. We tried to slip out, but they turned their attention to us, asking questions about our families. "It's only because you dedicated your novel to your grandparents that I took an interest in you in the first place," Lyda yelled. Frank started to boast of his descent from Lord Mansfield, who freed the slaves in England, and from Edward Doty, the only servant on the *Mayflower*. Lyda then berated her 'idiot' for having taken down the poster of Lenin on the back of the bathroom door. Apparently, when I'd told him that the friends who might join us lived in Brooklyn, Frank had assumed they'd be Jewish and, being Jewish, offended by the poster of Lenin. Frank saw us out, saying Lyda didn't understand how certain people who'd befriended her had ulterior motives.

When the phone rang the next morning I answered it at Julie's insistence. It was indeed Lyda, who said she wished to have lunch sometime soon with Julie alone. After she hung up, Julie and I agreed we'd gotten into a trap, like the poor guy at the end of Evelyn Waugh's *A Handful of Dust* who's forced to live out his days reading Dickens to a lunatic. In addition, we both recognized Frank and Lyda as grotesque parodies of ourselves, a nightmare vision of how we might turn out at their age if we weren't careful.

Lyda did not press Julie further for lunch, though she continued to phone with bits of news through the end of the summer – Frank had received a big royalty check from Arkham House, Frank's article in *Reign of Fear* (an anthology of essays on Stephen King) was the best in the volume. Then Frank called, to ask for a loan of fifty dollars. He subsequently picked up the money in an envelope I left with our doorman.

Lyda called to thank us for the loan, which she said they were prepared to repay the next time we met. I vowed we'd invite them to dinner soon. First, however, I saw to it that we had some support. Ted, loyal friend that he was, agreed to come and even offered to pick the Longs up in his car. I said that wouldn't be necessary since Lyda used some sort of service for invalids to drive her places. When I phoned the Longs, Lyda was delighted to accept. She promised to bring us the fifty dollars. Later Ted realized we'd chosen to entertain the night of the first presidential debate between Bush and Dukakis. Fortunately, though, he could tape it on his VCR.

The appointed evening Frank arrived at our apartment, like the Longs' a ground-floor rear one, around 7:30. He explained that they'd gotten off at the wrong address and Lyda was up the street, her wheelchair not working too well. Shortly after we retrieved Lyda and her wheelchair, Ted arrived, thank God. We ushered our guests into the living room, where everyone took a seat around the coffee table – Lyda in a chair next to Julie, Ted next to Frank on the couch. When I offered drinks, Lyda asked for straight vodka with a glass of orange juice on the side. (She never touched the orange juice.) Frank ordered Scotch. First Lyda did her show-and-tell routine – photos that Giles had taken at Frank's birthday, a collage or two, old newspaper clippings, mementos of the Yiddish theater, the lot. Frank told me he'd gone through most of my manuscript and had a few corrections to suggest. I said a friend of mine was reading his *Autobiographical Memoir* and enjoying it. "I'm contemplating writing a real, full-scale memoir in which I'll talk about all the famous people in the science fiction world I've known," he said. "This will be my big book, which will take care of all our financial needs for the rest of our days."

Lyda complimented us on our apartment, which as an artist Julie had spruced up considerably since our wedding, in large part through the addition of some of her own paintings. At one point, when I led Frank to the bathroom, he praised Julie's decorating taste. He was also impressed by our built-in bookshelves, and admitted he had few books in his own library. True to form Lyda started to hold forth on her pet peeves. Having consumed his Scotch, Frank fell into a stupor. Once or twice he roused himself to take exception to his better half's wackier pronouncements. We heard all the familiar tales again – Frank's resemblance to Dostoevsky's 'idiot', their courtship and marriage, the world's failure to appreciate her Frankele.

Shortly before we served dinner, Ted excused himself to go turn on his VCR. Since he lived only a few blocks away, he was back in time for the first course. The party moved into the dining room. Julie, as fine a cook as she was a decorator, had prepared a feast, which Frank proceeded to gobble up without comment, course after course, while the company endured Lyda's criticisms of Tom, of Kirby, of de Camp, of conventions, of horror writers in general. At moments Frank did dispute Lyda's more malicious slanders, but clearly he cared more about polishing his plate than arguing. After dessert the men returned to the living room, while Julie remained stuck at the table in a tête-à-tête with Lyda. (Julie later reported Lyda had revealed that she and Frank had had sex for three months after their wedding then stopped. She'd wanted a divorce but Frank refused to give it to her.)

Back on the couch Frank complained to Ted about the fast pace of modern life.

"You seem to have escaped the drudgery most people have to go through in their careers," said Ted, rather disingenuously, I thought. "How have you done it?"

Frank ignored the question. "We may be blown up in a nuclear war," he replied, "so nothing matters anyway."

Around 11:30 Julie and I decided the party was over. We helped our older guests, who seemed to be unaware of the time, with their coats and baggage. (Later we saw that we'd overlooked some of Lyda's photos.) Ted and I found a friendly cab driver, gave him fifteen bucks and instructions on taking the Longs home. As the cab sped off downtown, I turned to Ted in exasperation. What could we do to rid ourselves of these emotional parasites?

"Get them nice and comfortable," Ted said, "and tell them about the rabbits…"

XI

When Lyda phoned the next day to thank us, I felt a little less like shooting the Longs. "Your apartment is like a gallery," she said. "It's like the Louvre." Two days later when Lyda called, I told her Julie wasn't home when in fact she was. "Frank was wondering if Julie might be Jewish," she said. Three days later Lyda phoned to say she had a girl to introduce to Ted. "Please have Julie call me back." A month later Lyda left a message on our machine accusing me of not giving Julie her calls. A week after that she succeeded in reaching Julie and told her she considered her "one of my best friends." Julie gritted her teeth and promised they'd get together soon.

Early in December Frank spoke to Julie. He wished to see me. When I called back, Frank said Lyda had been in the hospital for blood tests. I said Julie had been ill. "I've been under a lot of pressure," he said, "but I wanted to give you some background on Alfred Galpin and Clark Ashton Smith pertaining to slips you made in your study." Galpin and Smith had been friends of Lovecraft's. On the whole my manuscript had impressed Frank. "Did Mosig write the first part?" he asked, Mosig having been one of those under contract who had not delivered. No, I said, I wrote the entire thing. "I'll pay back the money I owe you when we next get together," he said. Apparently he hadn't been able to get down to the shop in the Village where he sometimes sold his more valuable books. I promised I'd call him again in a couple of weeks.

The following day Frank left a message on our machine. Lyda was worried about Julie's health, given what I had told him. In fact Julie's ailment had been minor. Lyda later left a message expressing her concern. Two days later Lyda called again, wanting to talk to Julie. I said she was asleep. She got through to Julie a few days before Christmas, to invite us to dinner. A subsequent message on our machine the same day reneged on the invitation. We thanked our lucky stars. The final day of the year Lyda called and again spoke to Julie. Frank had woken up in the night and didn't know where he was. She was very worried.

Early in January Lyda phoned. "Guess what?" she said. "A Providence TV station wants to interview Frank, but they won't get very far unless they pay." I asked to speak to Frank. "I'm expecting to get a check soon so I can repay you," he said. I said I'd forget the debt if he'd agree to write a jacket blurb for my Lovecraft study. A sentence or two was all I required. "I'll give you a paragraph," he replied. He had the usual fifteen or sixteen things to deal with but would do it soon.

A week or so later Lyda called back. "I've been after Frank to write a blurb for your book," she said. Kirby's sister had just sent them a hundred dollars in cash, but she was sure it was some sort of ploy.

Thinking I'd waited long enough, I called Frank to arrange to pick up the blurb. (I didn't trust him to dictate it over the phone.) Within seconds he launched into a tirade – about the value of his time, his early letters selling for hundreds of dollars and his getting nothing and other outrages. On my lunch hour the following day I went over to their place, only to discover that the 'blurb' – it had expanded to two pages – wasn't ready. The trip wasn't a total waste, however. I returned the photographs they'd left behind at our apartment, and I saw that at last they had a working refrigerator. The kitchen was painted and cleaned up. Perhaps life was getting better for them after all. Before I left Lyda showed me a black-and-blue mark on her leg where she said Frank had kicked her.

I scheduled another gathering at the Longs'. Julie begged off and ST in effect went in her place. Frank met us at the door. "Having spent the afternoon with Kirby, I would've preferred to call the evening off," he said, "but Lyda had everything set." Again I was struck by how tidy the apartment looked. In the living room Lyda was lying on her bed. A tray of liquor bottles and paper cups rested on the floor. ST and I helped ourselves to peach schnapps. I poured a cup of vodka for Lyda. She proceeded to hold forth on India and famous Indians she had known, while Frank retired to his room. When he returned, after some fifteen minutes, Lyda was telling us Kirby was in bad shape. "Everything's fine with Kirby," Frank said, though I later heard from Ted that Kirby had lost Stephen King as a client. Lyda praised Kay, Kirby's sister, for her generosity. Frank showed us the French edition of *Dreamer*, which ST said he'd mention in the next issue of *Lovecraft Studies*.

It proved to be one of the easier visits with the Longs. Frank was not his usual agitated or gloomy self – he seemed actually relaxed and even smiled. The banter between him and Lyda was almost good-natured. Frank spoke of earning hundreds of thousands from his prospective memoir about all the science fiction greats he had known over the years. A TV crew was coming down from Providence to interview him about Lovecraft. It was Poe's birthday that day, we remembered, his 180th.

After about an hour I finally asked Frank if he was ready to give me his 'review'. He said he'd finished his 'introduction', though he still had some marginal notes to make on the manuscript. I said the marginal notes could wait. Frank disappeared and came back with two handwritten sheets of typewriter bond. "I cut it down from four," he said. "It's titled 'Introductory Comment.'" When I explained that the series editor had already written a foreword to the book, hence I had no need of another introductory piece, Frank seemed a trifle miffed. It was a good moment for ST and me to make our escape.

The first sentence of 'Introductory Comment' was quintessential Long: 'In appraising a biography of someone who played as important a role in my life as HP Lovecraft my first and immediate reaction is likely to be of a generalized nature.' Ho hum – but to my joy the text went uphill from there, impeded only by the occasional awkward phrase or infelicitous word choice. It was both highly complimentary and insightful. I derived from it the jacket blurb I'd requested in the first place, while the complete text ran as a prepublication review in the spring issue of *Lovecraft Studies*.

In the days that followed I typed up a transcript of Frank's text, correcting minor errors, and sent a copy to my editor at Twayne. Lyda called asking for Julie. I lied and said she wasn't home. I mailed Frank a postal card thanking him for his review. Lyda phoned again.

"The TV crew caused a great stir yesterday," she said. "They spent nearly four hours with Frank interviewing him for a documentary in honor of the centenary." I knew plans to celebrate Lovecraft's centennial year were already in the works. Brett, a friend of theirs who'd recently moved to New Jersey from Providence, had been present. Brett was a talented poet.

On Valentine's Day we arrived home late to find a frantic message from Lyda on our machine. Frank had been having seizures and was in a bad way. I called back and spoke to someone who I assumed was a paramedic. He reported that Frank refused to go to the hospital. Half an hour later Lyda phoned again, sounding extremely upset. Frank had been taken to St. Vincent's.

XII

Three days later Julie phoned Lyda, who told her Frank had pneumonia and phlebitis. The cause of his seizures was unknown. When I next spoke to Lyda, she said I should go visit Frank the following day. He had a correction for me. I promised to stop at the hospital after work.

When I arrived at St. Vincent's Frank was asleep. He was hooked up to an IV and assorted monitoring equipment. A nurse was in the room. A delivery man arrived with flowers, which turned out to be from Kirby and Kay. After a minute Frank woke up. "Everyone's gone," he muttered. "Fifteen or so." I moved closer to his bedside. As soon as he gained full consciousness, he started to tell me about an error I'd have to fix in my book. "You got Loveman's age wrong," he said. "You called him a young protégé when he was nearly Lovecraft's own age." I later checked. Frank was right.

I asked him how he was doing. He said the doctors would be testing him to find out why his vision was distorted. He had to keep lying horizontally. "I hope to get out in a week," he said, "though it could be a lot longer." The nurse picked up the phone when it rang. It was Lyda. Frank got on the line and told her he was okay. When I got on she asked me to call her later. "She has several friends to come in and look after her needs," Frank said. "I don't want her going into my room. I have everything arranged just so." I said I'd do what I could to help her. After about twenty minutes I left, promising to return soon. When I got home I called Lyda. She was worried that the doctors didn't know what was wrong. "Please stay in touch," she said.

I called my editor, who said there was time in production to change Loveman from a 'young protégé' to an 'early amateur associate'. Two days later I spent an hour and a half with Frank, who seemed less with it than before. It was hard to understand his words, but mostly he seemed to be complaining about the agony he'd been going through. A nurse gave him some pills and he drowsed off. Frank coughed now and then, but the nurse said that was good. Kay called. She said she spoke to Lyda daily. I gathered she was looking after things in general. Since Frank wanted his condition kept quiet, she hadn't informed the science fiction community at large. As for Frank's illness, she pointed out that only a relative could find out what was really going on. Frank raised his hand in a feeble wave when I left. I phoned Lyda to give her an update. That he seemed unchanged didn't strike her as good.

About a week later, on my next hospital visit, Frank was sleeping. He looked better – and actually cleaner than he'd probably been in years. The IV was gone. A set of slippers by his bedside suggested he could walk. Soon after I got home that evening, Lyda phoned. She was feeling terrible and needed help getting to the hospital. Despite the imminent arrival of dinner guests, I agreed to go down to their apartment. Julie could cope on her own. The subway got me there as fast as a cab would have by eight o'clock. Lyda was evidently suffering a spell of depression. She'd tried phoning all her friends but only I was around. She apologized for pulling me away from my party.

"I don't want to go to St. Vincent's," she said. Her voice was subdued. "I'll just have to wait up all night in the emergency ward and possibly not even be admitted since there's nothing physically wrong with me." Her doctor, who was Frank's doctor, couldn't be reached until the morning because he was at a party. "Please let me come stay with you," she pleaded. I explained the situation, how it would be awkward with guests at our place, how we simply couldn't put her up for the night. I phoned Julie, who was of a like mind. Lyda asked to speak to her, but Julie was off the line before Lyda took the receiver. We discussed alternatives. In the end she agreed that the best thing was for her to stay at home. At her request I went out and got her two cups of black coffee. "I'm terribly sorry," she kept repeating. "I must let you go." I was home by ten, in time to catch the end of dinner.

At a gang gathering the second week of March, I heard about Frank from others. Bob, who'd recently moved back to New Jersey from North Carolina, said the publisher he'd approached wasn't interested in doing an entire book on Frank – maybe a chapter in a volume covering several writers. Brett said the people from Providence who interviewed Frank were amateurs who hoped a television station might buy their film. Frank had been quite cranky during the interview, but after an hour had settled down.

When I next visited Frank, he'd been moved to a double room. He was wearing his glasses and looked healthy but was still on his back. Lyda was there, and we chatted in the hall while Frank's roommate was x-rayed. "Frank very much needs visitors," she said. "Giles comes by most evenings." I sat alone with Frank, but we didn't have much of a conversation. He complained of pain in his legs, from lying too long in the same position. He rolled briefly on his side. He talked a little about Bush's politics. He'd been taken for a long walk earlier in the day. Both Frank and Lyda said they'd been asked all sorts of questions by social workers. Frank spoke of starving writers – of the Irishman dying in the streets of Dublin while a play of his was a Broadway hit. Since it was a warm day, Frank rested on top of the covers. I noticed that his bare feet were dry, red, scaly, almost reptilian.

A week later, when I stopped by the hospital, Frank was screaming at Lyda because she'd failed to bring a get-well card from home. She said she forgot it. Frank was sure she was hiding something from him. He was mad that his beard had been shaved off. In fact, he had a half-inch left on his chin. At Lyda's prompting, I said he looked fine.

I gave Frank an envelope, marked 'from a fan'. It was an anonymous gift of fifty dollars from Bob's parents that Bob had passed on to me. He was thrilled. (Later I told Lyda the source of the cash.) Then he started complaining about the black woman who had given him a shower. "I'm deathly afraid of blacks," he said. (Black people who were strangers it might be fairer to say, since he betrayed no fear of Giles in my presence.) "Koch is loyal first to Israel," he added, speaking of the city's mayor. Soon he was bragging of his own exalted lineage, as a *Mayflower* and Lord Mansfield descendant. And for the nth time he chastised me for calling his style old-fashioned. And for the nth time I confessed and bewailed my manifold sin. "Joshi gets things right four-fifths of the time," he said, "but the rest of the time..."

I conferred with Lyda in the hall. The problem was that the hospital wanted to discharge Frank, which probably meant his going into a nursing home. "He can't get around by himself," she said. "What are we to do?"

On my next visit I brought, at Lyda's suggestion, a copy of the Sunday *Daily News*. Frank was glad to have the tabloid, since the *New York Times* wouldn't have been as entertaining. On the whole he seemed in good spirits. He had no complaints – except about a new error he'd spotted in my Lovecraft study. In the bibliography I'd accidentally cited Necronomicon Press instead of Arkham House as the publisher of *Dreamer on the Nightside*. I was wrong again... Frank acted more alert, less drugged than before, and his voice was stronger. He had plenty of magazines to read. He gave me a page from the *Times*, an article about a literary tour, illustrated by a cartoon sketch of Poe, Whitman, and Melville walking together. He wanted me to get the picture copied so he could send it to a couple of his correspondents. When dinner arrived two nurses helped him sit up. I read the paper while he ate. An operation on his prostate a few days earlier had gone well – the next day the doctors would deal with his hernia. Before I left, Frank said he was grateful I'd come to see him.

That night I spoke to Lyda. Frank had had a stroke and could no longer walk unaided, though he didn't know it yet. "His personality has changed too," she said. "He's now less shy, much more assertive." She'd been putting off the social worker who wanted to see their apartment. They'd need someone to stay with them full-time. She didn't trust Kay anymore, since Kay hadn't been so helpful of late.

On my next trip to the hospital I encountered Lyda in the hall outside Frank's room. The hernia operation was a success, but now he'd caught double pneumonia. Frank was obviously not as well as when I'd seen him last. He was back on the IV. I passed on a copy of the latest *Lovecraft Studies*, courtesy of ST. He read it for a little while with interest, but it was clear he was in discomfort if not actual pain. He was in no state to hold a conversation.

I visited Frank again the day before his birthday and gave him back the picture of Poe, Whitman, and Melville, with photocopies. Both Frank and Lyda commented that the one magazine to be taken from his bedside collection was *Lovecraft Studies*. They said they'd like another copy at some point.

A week later Lyda phoned. "Guess what?" she said. "Ray Bradbury has sent Frank a check for five hundred dollars!" An appeal had gone out and the money would soon be rolling in. Even better, she reported there was a good chance Frank would be able to walk with rehabilitation. A subsequent call from Lyda was a mistake. "I thought I was dialing Ben," she said. Ben, she made clear, was the one who was spreading the word about Frank to the big shots in the horror world. The social worker had told her they could set up a hospital bed for Frank at home. Lyda sounded optimistic, like her old grandiose self again.

When I next saw Frank he confirmed that Lyda had come out of her depression. He himself was in good form, grousing about the black attendants. He needed to be repositioned after physical therapy, but we decided it was best for the nurse to do it, not me. I brought him a box of Kleenex from the neighboring bed, which was unoccupied, for his cough. He was off the IV. A woman screamed from the next room. "She does it all day," said Frank, implying it was no big deal.

A week later I rescued Julie from another one of Lyda's pestering calls. "I'm expecting ten thousand dollars from Stephen King!" she proclaimed when I got on the line. Frank would be home in two weeks. But Frank would remain in the hospital at least another month and my visits to him there continued.

In mid-May when I saw him Frank commented in awe on how strong his black nurse was. When Brett arrived, the three of us discussed Poe, Sarah Helen Whitman, and 'The Bells'. Frank corrected Brett on some detail in a poem of his about Poe and Mrs. Whitman. Lyda appeared, bedecked in green turban and matching earrings. When Frank started to complain that he was choking and Lyda was ignoring him, I decided it was time to leave.

The first week of June Lyda called to vent her anger at L Sprague de Camp, with whom it appeared she had spoken. "He claimed he was broke because he'd just moved to Texas and his wife was in the hospital," she said. "I let him have it. I told him how vulgar I thought he was, the way he behaved at conventions." Somehow I couldn't imagine that dignified gentleman carrying on as some younger immature attendees did at conventions. Lyda was sure he was rich from all the books he'd published. When I visited Frank the next day he was worried that Lyda hadn't shown up or called. "Probably out shopping," he muttered.

The first day of summer Lyda phoned and spoke to Julie -- Frank was coming home at last and we were invited to come celebrate.

XIII

Julie declined to join the celebration, but bought some flowers for me to bring to Frank. Despite being unable to reach the Longs by phone earlier in the day to confirm, I decided to show up at the hour originally set. ST was free to join me. Though we arrived on the early side, our hosts didn't seem to mind. At the door we had to be careful not to let their new pet, a friendly little mongrel named Drushka, escape. Lyda had told Julie she didn't want ST to come because he hadn't visited Frank in the hospital, but her manner towards him was entirely cordial.

Frank was lying in a hospital bed set up in the living room. I raised the head of it for him. Lyda provided drinks. She and I each had a beer, while ST had a glass of wine. I handed Frank a glass of orange juice – and his copy of *HP Lovecraft*, my critical study, which had just been published. Mumbling that he was disgusted with the whole situation, Frank didn't respond, other than to berate me for attributing *Dreamer on the Nightside* to Necronomicon Press instead of Arkham House. "You didn't even read it!" he yelled.

Iris arrived, the Jamaican nurse who had the night shift. Lyda told her how much she liked Jamaican rum. In French she confided to us that Frank, like Lovecraft, detested blacks. I hoped that Iris, like Frank, didn't understand French. I left after less than an hour, since I had to go meet Julie. ST stayed. Brett was due to show at any moment. A few days later Lyda phoned to say that Brett and Giles had dropped in after my departure. "What an intellectual conversation they had!" she gushed.

In July Lyda roped us into attending a party in honor of their new dog. Since she said there'd be seven other guests, we decided it wouldn't be too bad. Brett greeted Julie and me at the door. We gave Drushka a chew toy, a rubber bird, in which he showed almost no interest. Frank was stretched out in the hospital bed, looking well, though he didn't at first recognize Julie. Julie accepted a glass of wine, I a beer. Frank drank orange juice. As usual Lyda held forth, but this time it was largely in praise of Brett. She read a poem from one of his collections that he'd given the Longs. In addition, she shared the same letters, collages, and photocopied materials we'd seen so often in the past.

Frank contributed little to the conversation, other than to worry that Lyda had invited too many people. "Fifteen you told me," he said to her. Then he was disappointed when no one else appeared. We three were in fact the only guests. In the kitchen Brett heated up some turkey and stuffing and a baked potato for Frank. After about two hours the three of us left, agreeing that the evening could have been a lot worse.

Through the rest of the summer Lyda phoned, leaving messages when we were out: "Kay has sent us a check for reprint rights to one of Frank's stories... Columbia University has invited Frank to speak... A French organization wants Frank to join a group of horror writers gathering in honor of Lovecraft's hundredth... Frank's now using a walker, but he needs intellectual stimulation. You should round up Joshi and the others and visit... I want to introduce Ted to a couple of available women."

In September I finally succumbed and organized yet another expedition to the Longs, but this time we had a small group, including Brett, ST and his fiancée Leslie. When the four of us arrived, Lyda complained that they had no home attendant that day. In any event, she tended to dismiss them early because they never did much. I helped Frank sit in his wheelchair and change his shirt. Lyda offered refreshments – beer, orange juice, which Brett brought, cheese and salami. As at the start of every such occasion, Lyda did all the talking. When she announced that she was going to stop, Frank piped up, "I hope so."

Brett tried to explain that there was no reason for her to feel miffed because Frank hadn't been included in a breakfast where three science fiction writers would be speaking over the weekend as part of the annual New York Is Book Country fair. Nor should she be put out because Frank's books weren't being sold at the festivities. Lyda said Ted never called her back when she left a message about setting him up. She complimented Leslie on her appearance, and remarked what a bad dresser she thought Brett was when she first knew him. Since ST was sitting in a corner behind Frank's wheelchair, it took Frank an hour to realize he was present. Julie arrived late, having missed nothing.

On the Longs' living room wall was a pencil portrait of Lovecraft, an excellent likeness, by an artist fan who had recently sent it as a gift. This same fan had mailed ST his copy of *Dreamer on the Nightside*, and ST now took the opportunity to get it signed. Frank, however, misunderstood and inscribed the book 'For Joshie' *(sic)*. When this error was brought to his attention, Frank told ST, "If you want to, you can write his name over yours." Frank's handwriting was pretty shaky. "Maybe he won't notice the difference." The artist's name was 'Steve'.

Giles appeared, shortly before Frank started to squirm in his wheelchair. I was close enough to hear Lyda whisper "Is it one or two?" and to hear his reply – 'b.m.' At Lyda's direction we younger guests retired to the hall while she and Giles attended to Frank. When we returned Frank was in bed, looking more comfortable. It seemed the moment to leave, but Lyda insisted we stay another fifteen minutes. When we finally did get away, she said how important it was for Frank that we had all come.

XIV

The week before Thanksgiving Lyda called and spoke to Julie. She never wanted to see us again. When we returned from Thanksgiving in Massachusetts, there was a message on our machine from Lyda forgiving me. "I never forget a kindness," she said, "your staying up with me that night." Another message was from ST about getting together with the representative for an Italian publishing house who was in town and wanted to meet Frank. Julie insisted that this time I avoid the Longs. I phoned ST and gave him what I believed was their current number to pass on to Giuseppe, the Italian visitor. When Lyda called a few days later to invite us to a party for Giuseppe the following evening, I said I was sorry, we couldn't make it. The next week Lyda reported that the evening didn't come off because their phone had been out of order.

A week later I spoke again with Lyda. "I'm planning a party for Frank and I want the names of Lovecraftians I don't know to invite," she said. She was going to bring to New York Brett's play about HPL and his wife Sonia. (It had been staged in Providence, I knew.) Returning from a weekend in Connecticut, we found several messages from Lyda on our machine, including one that lasted minutes because she'd failed to hang up the receiver properly. After she stopped talking we could hear the TV humming and Frank quietly griping.

I decided to pay the Longs a surprise visit the next day. As it turned out, they had guests that evening. Kay, whom I was pleased to meet finally face to face, had brought over an old friend of Frank's, Julius Schwartz, who was famous among Lovecraftians for having agented as a teen-ager one of HPL's major tales the year before his death. "It was at a party in the Village," he said. "I just went up to Lovecraft and introduced myself and asked if he had any unplaced stories." For once I was truly annoyed by Lyda's dominating the conversation, since I had little chance to talk with 'Julie', who was obviously a charming and witty man. He referred to Frank as 'Belknap', the name people called him in his youth to distinguish him from his father, Frank, Sr. I showed him Frank's copy of my new book, though I was a bit embarrassed when he couldn't find himself in the index. (Later I saw that I'd mentioned him but not by name.)

When Julie started to tell me about how he and Belknap used to meet with other writers once a week in the Village in the forties, Lyda interrupted with a rant about how Frank had been exploited. "I haven't been exploited!" screamed Frank from his wheelchair, hitherto all but silent. Then Lyda started attacking Kirby – which didn't go over well with Kay. In the background the Hispanic home attendant giggled.

Finally, probably sensing nobody really cared to listen to her, Lyda delivered her show-stopper. She turned to Schwartz and asked, "Do you want to fuck?" Julie hadn't been afraid to talk back to Lyda earlier, but even he was at a loss for a snappy reply to this one. Lyda repeated her request. While he and Kay didn't leave immediately, a pall settled over the party from which it never recovered. Frank summoned enough energy to criticize me for not including *The Early Long* in my bibliography. I said I'd listed it in *Pulptime*. Lyda said Joseph Papp was going to produce Brett's Lovecraft play. "I'm playing Sonia!"

When it came my turn to depart, Lyda gave me a present for my Julie – a shell necklace with matching purse. She assured me it was worth two hundred dollars.

For the rest of the month Lyda bombarded us with messages. "Julius Schwartz called to say he'd like me to be his mistress," she initially reported, though he evidently hadn't left his number, for in trying to reach him through information she'd talked to some other Schwartz, a Russian immigrant, who in the end offered to translate Frank's books. She phoned Kay to tell her the great news, but Kay was too busy to listen. "You call Kay and tell her," she said. Frank translated into Russian, the ultimate triumph, but I ignored her. One message told us to go to hell for not giving her presents – another that Frank had broken from Kirby. "I'm Frank's agent now!" As for her propositioning Julius Schwartz, she said she'd done it to liven things up.

In January the tune changed. She told Julie she was going into the hospital. When I called back she sounded calm. She was concerned about Frank being left alone. Later she informed us that she was too anemic to be operated on – for what she didn't say. Near the end of the month we received a letter stating 'I have gifted you royally' and accusing us of giving her nothing in return. Under her signature she had written 'Grâce à Dieu I am not a Lousecraftian'. Julie and I seriously discussed severing all ties with the Longs.

When Lyda next called, I angrily told her we had our own lives and to stop bugging us. Her tone was conciliatory. She urged me to come visit Frank. When I phoned a few days later, she said because she had the flu I would have to postpone my visit. She was grateful I'd called. The following week she phoned again. Frank had fallen and was in the hospital, but fortunately he'd broken no bones. The first anniversary of his seizure loomed. Julie took her next call. Frank was coming home and she expected us to bring over a bottle of champagne to celebrate on Valentine's. On the 14th we were occupied with a personal crisis of our own. The following day Julie listened as Lyda left an irate message on our machine. With my approval Julie wrote Lyda a letter saying we wanted nothing more to do with her, but leaving the door open for me to see Frank.

The last weekend of the month there was a gang gathering in the Village. After the usual bookstore sweep, Bob and I dropped by the Longs'. Frank was stretched out on the living room couch. The hospital bed was gone. While Bob chatted with Frank, Lyda apologized to me. They were desperate. Since Brett had moved back to Providence, there was no one around to visit on a regular basis. I promised to bring over a larger contingent of Lovecraftians the next time. Frank speculated on the relative intelligence of whites and blacks. At Lyda's request I walked the dog.

XV

In late March, the afternoon of Julie's birthday, I visited the Longs. I had called in advance and they were expecting me. The home attendant opened the door. In the living room Frank was in his wheelchair watching a soap opera on TV, while Lyda was sitting in a corner with the dog. Frank didn't greet me until Lyda made a point of calling my presence to his attention.

Lyda praised the home attendant, Elizabeth, who had now been with them three months. "She washes Frank everywhere," she said, "even his tiny penis." Elizabeth, a Puerto Rican woman, had her post in the alcove outside the kitchen, where she sat watching a mini-TV. From the way she handled the Longs that afternoon I could tell Elizabeth was a loving person with a good sense of humor – they were indeed lucky to have her. "She kisses Frank when she bathes him," Lyda added. "Like a baby."

Lyda took a couple of pictures with her new Polaroid camera – one of me talking to Frank, the other of me holding Drushka with Frank to the side. She gave me the first photo, as well as a hardcover copy of Stephen King's novel *The Dark Half*, which she said she'd bought on the street for $1.50. (After reading it I got about the same price for it from a used-book buyer.) Her old cheap camera, she explained, had been stolen by someone who'd offered to get her a cab.

Lyda complained that her teeth couldn't be fixed (she was missing her front two) because she was too anemic. She'd recently received a legacy of eight hundred dollars, from a friend who'd died in 1978, so they were better off financially than they'd been. She asked if Julie had gotten over her anger. She clearly valued Julie's good opinion. Frank looked reasonably well. He'd been walking a little with his walker. "I find it astonishing," he said, "that a person could win two big lotteries. A math professor says the odds are only about one in thirty of such an event happening." Maybe the math professor meant thirty thousand – or thirty million. Frank smiled at the dog, even laughed, as the animal played at his feet. It was the only time I saw Frank laughing aloud.

Lyda chided Frank on their sex life. "You said you had a big erection last night," she said. "I want you to fuck me" – when you're well enough to do so, she seemed to be suggesting.

"Don't use such language," Frank replied.

This exchange led Frank to comment on what a gentleman Lovecraft was. "His grandfather's library of nineteenth-century books made all the difference," he said. Actually, it was his grandfather's eighteenth-century books that HPL regarded as a strong formative influence. "Only once did Howard ever revise my poetry," Frank continued, "changing a line because it disparaged a career in business." After all, Whipple Phillips, Lovecraft's maternal grandfather, had been both a cultured man and a man of affairs. Frank's grandfather Doty had been a bigwig connected with the Waldorf Hotel.

"Lovecraft was a homosexual!" Lyda proclaimed.

"No he wasn't!" Frank retorted.

"That's why Sonia left him!"

"You have it all wrong. Howard was not a homosexual!"

"Well, maybe a quarter or an eighth."

Frank changed the subject – to my failing to list *The Early Long* in my Lovecraft study. "You misattributed it to Arkham House instead of Doubleday," he whined. It appeared he was confusing my sin of omission, neglecting to cite *The Early Long*, with my sin of commission, crediting *Dreamer on the Nightside* to Necronomicon Press instead of Arkham House.

Lyda said Frank had a trunk full of papers he wanted to go through, but he couldn't do it alone. Brett was going to help, before he moved. I offered to assist instead, though I doubted he'd preserved any real treasures. Lyda was aware that the forthcoming HPL centennial in Providence was an important event. She wondered why Joshi was such a big shot. I said ST was universally acknowledged as the world's leading Lovecraft scholar. (She wasn't surprised when I told her he was no longer engaged.) In June the Horror Writers of America would be holding their annual meeting in Providence in honor of the centenary. Lyda planned to get on a panel and tell everyone off for neglecting Frank. Frank remembered how the young Isaac Asimov once came up to him and told him that he, Frank, was one of his heroes.

Lyda in her turn waxed nostalgic. "I remember how I first saw Frank in his Brooklyn apartment," she said, "with his cat walking on the ceiling. So innocent, so unassuming."

"No I'm not unassuming!" Frank protested. "What do you mean unassuming?" That she'd claimed his cat had been "walking on the ceiling" didn't seem to be an issue for dispute.

Lyda moved next to Frank. "He needs to be with intellectuals," she said, stroking his hair. "I'm not one." She asked Frank to recite some of his poetry. On cue he declaimed 'Sonnet' ('The gods are dead...') and a stanza from 'In Mayan Splendor'. A few tears rolled down Lyda's cheek.

"Frank's family has a plot in Woodlawn in the Bronx," she said gently. "One day he'll be buried there."

"Well, it won't be long now," Frank muttered.

The tenderness didn't last. Soon they were back on Lovecraft. "Lovecraft hated blacks and Jews and so does Frank!" Lyda roared. "This one black hospital attendant was especially frightening to Frank. You should have heard him. If only we had a tape-recorder!" How I wished I'd brought a tape-recorder!

So passed perhaps the most outrageous, certainly the most affecting, visit with the Longs since they entertained me and Julie in their hall. Again emotions had run high, but this time there'd been a redeeming element – a real display of love, at least on Lyda's part. One had to give her credit for that, as I later told Julie over her birthday dinner.

Almost two months went by before we heard again from Lyda. She was depressed. She was afraid she'd have to go into the hospital, where she'd soon die. Then Frank would have to go into a home, which he'd never survive. "You've been our one constant friend," she said. I promised to keep in touch.

Three days later, after consulting Lyda, I stopped in for an hour. Frank looked well. He said Mondadori, the Italian publisher, was reprinting *Rim of the Unknown*, his second Arkham House story collection, and paying him four thousand dollars. If true, he had good reason to be cheerful. He showed me a batch of recent fan mail. One fan had written a complimentary letter that asked nothing for himself. Another wanted Frank to autograph some gummed labels he'd enclosed. Lyda was subdued, letting Frank do the talking. It was in the depth of her depression that she was the most considerate of others. Frank said he worried about her in her current condition. Nonetheless, he was optimistic he would make it to the Lovecraft Centennial Conference that summer.

XVI

When I spoke with Lyda in May, she said she thought she'd put Frank on a bus to Providence for the conference, accompanied by a home attendant. I was sure we could do better than that. On my next visit I told them Bob would be driving from New Jersey and might be able to give them a ride. They showed me a letter from the librarian in charge of coordinating speakers for the weekend, which was sponsored by Brown University's John Hay Library, home to a vast collection of Lovecraft's papers, and supported in part by a grant from the state of Rhode Island arts council. The organizers were aware that Frank was among the more distinguished Lovecraft authorities to be invited (certainly the most venerable), and had offered him a room at the university's guest house.

Lyda said she'd been corresponding with relatives in Russia who hoped to emigrate to Israel. Frank burbled about his illustrious ancestors. Lyda asked me to go through Frank's manuscript trunk sometime after the conference. The radio was turned on to the Saturday afternoon opera. Frank said he liked classical music but not opera, a preference I said I shared.

Frank could now walk outside, though he was quite unsteady when he got up and grabbed his walker in the living room. "When I first knew Lovecraft he looked ten years older than his actual age," Frank remarked. "You look ten years younger." Lyda questioned me more about myself than usual. She admitted she'd just come out of a three-month depression. Before I left, she gave me a copy of the *Chelsea Clinton News*, a neighborhood paper. She wanted me to prepare a piece for it on Frank and the conference.

When later that day I proposed to Bob that he drive the Long entourage up to Providence, he declined the honor. He had other passengers, driving into the city was a hassle, the luggage might not all fit. And, while Bob didn't say so, he could imagine as well as I could that traveling eight hours to Providence and back with the aged couple would be no picnic. I had my own excellent excuse – Julie and I would be vacationing in Little Compton, Rhode Island, the week immediately beforehand. Nonetheless, I knew that if Frank was to make it to the Lovecraft Centennial Conference, I had to be the one to ensure that it happened.

Lyda called several times over the next few days. Once she reached Julie while Julie was on the other line and refused to get off. She liked the idea of being driven to Providence. She would pay me to sort through Frank's papers. Frank had received a check for $36,000. Frank had seen a doctor who told him he was too thin at a hundred pounds. In the meantime I spoke to Jenny, the Brown librarian, who promised to look into providing wheelchairs at their end. It would be better for the Longs to stay at a motel since the guest house had stairs.

As word spread of the Longs' situation, more than one Lovecraftian came forward to offer his help in paying for the rental of a van to transport them to Providence. This seemed the most sensible solution. Now all we needed was a chauffeur. There was one obvious candidate – Stefan Dziemianowicz. Stefan, a relative newcomer to our local Lovecraft circle, had never met the Longs. Like a boy scout, he was, I sensed, brave and trustworthy. Assuming the role of the commanding officer forced to select a 'volunteer' for the hazardous if not suicidal mission, I asked Stefan if he would get the job done. He accepted without hesitation.

When Lyda next called, I told her I'd lined up Stefan to drive them to Providence. I'd arrange a meeting with him soon. When I asked whether a home attendant was free to go with them, Lyda said they'd be taking along a 'secretary'. It was impossible to get a straight answer from her, now that she was in her latest manic phase. "I've just won a trip to China and Russia," she said when she phoned two days later. "I'll have to leave Frank in Brett's care in Providence."

The last day of July, Stefan and I met after work and walked over to the Longs'. On the way I filled Stefan in on what to expect. Frank and Lyda were waiting for us on the sidewalk in front of 421, in their wheelchairs. Standing beside them was a home attendant, a young Nigerian woman, who seemed friendly and kind. Frank was wearing a striped shirt with flowing cravat. Someone had obviously decided he should be looking his best for the occasion. Frank got up and walked in a circle using his walker, with a confidence and strength not evident my previous visit. A cloudburst drove us inside. We regrouped in the lobby.

Lyda took drink orders. The home attendant brought me a Cherry Coke from the apartment, then went to fetch beers for Frank and Stefan from the corner store. She said she was willing to accompany her charges to Providence, and seemed relieved when I told her it would only be for a weekend. I discussed logistics with Lyda. She thought the vehicle that had recently delivered Frank to the hospital for his check-up could take them to Providence. I said this was an unlikely option. Frank, as I later heard from Stefan, complained to him about a new anthology of Cthulhu Mythos fiction. The order of the stories made it appear as if Clark Ashton Smith had written the first non-Lovecraft tale in this vein, when in fact he Frank had done so, with 'The Space Eaters'.

After about forty-five minutes of this, Stefan and I were ready to go. I gave Lyda a paragraph I'd written about Frank and the conference for the *Chelsea Clinton News*, where as far as I know it never ran. Frank had one last thing on his mind. "That story of yours in *Crypt*," he said, speaking of 'The Appreciative Puritan', a tale of mine with a Lovecraft-like protagonist, a lame attempt at women's magazine fiction, fit only for Bob's zine. "You got Howard's character all wrong. He never would've said and done the things you have him say and do." I suppose I should have been grateful Frank was willing to share his critical comments.

The following day I phoned Lyda to tell her to expect Stefan on Friday the 17th for the drive up to Rhode Island. She subsequently left a string of short, incoherent messages – great things were happening, she was going to be on TV. In her present state I realized Lyda could make a real nuisance of herself at the conference. This wasn't just another 'con' (convention) but a serious academic tribute to Lovecraft. A number of foreign scholars would be coming, from France, Germany, and Italy, countries where, in contrast to the United States, HPL had a reputation outside the genre as an important author. Would they want their weekend marred by Lyda's antics? Why, for that matter, should she spoil the weekend for anyone? One Lovecraftian in Providence, a psychiatric doctor who treated psychotics, offered half in jest to have her committed on arrival.

I conferred with Kay. She said she'd never set foot in the Longs' place again after that evening Lyda insulted Julius Schwartz – who would never go back either. Frank's friends all avoided him when they came to town on her account. In the past Lyda had checked into hotels, including the Plaza and the Chelsea, and racked up huge bills. (They'd thrown her permanently out of the Chelsea, the landmark hotel on West 23rd that traditionally welcomed struggling writers and artists.) For now, thanks to the two hundred dollars or so Kirby gave them every month on top of their social security, the Longs had enough to live on. Kay was in touch with their doctors (Lyda had medication but refused to take it) and the home-care people. I described the suffering Lyda had caused Julie.

After talking with Kay I decided that ideally Lyda should remain in New York while Frank and the home attendant made the journey to Providence. I called Kay back to tell her so. As long as Stefan had one or two other able-bodied persons along to restrain her, he could haul Frank off and leave her behind. On the other hand, such strong-arm tactics might upset Frank. Better would be to give them some advance notice, to prepare them for the idea. Kay agreed it was worth a try, though if Lyda insisted Stefan would have to bring her too.

I felt better when Stefan told me he'd recruited Scott, another one of our local group, for the drive. The day Julie and I left for Little Compton, I mailed Lyda a letter politely but firmly suggesting that everyone, herself included, would be happier if she stayed home.

XVII

Friday evening of the conference, at the welcoming reception at the John Hay Library, I heard that both Frank and Lyda were coming. My letter had succeeded only in angering Lyda. Was she going to remain quietly at home when she had a chance to bask in Frank's reflected glory and have her say before a large audience? I'd been a fool to think there'd been the remotest possibility. At least I wasn't the one in charge of coping with her that weekend. Other Lovecraftians could have their turn.

I ran into Stefan and Scott at the registration desk after the reception. They both looked shell-shocked. They'd just come from dropping off the Longs at the Days Inn. The trip had been a nightmare. When they arrived at ten that morning Frank was still in bed. It took Lyda two and a half hours to pack – virtually her entire wardrobe it would seem, a dozen bags and suitcases. She brought her guitar because she said she'd arranged with Jenny to sing as part of the program. Whether any home attendant had been present wasn't clear. At any rate, none accompanied them. With the delayed departure they encountered terrible traffic on the interstate.

The program of panel discussions commenced Saturday morning, at Brown's University Hall. Julie left just as we spotted Stefan pulling up in the rented van with the Longs. She was to visit her parents overnight outside Boston and return the next day. Frank was scheduled to appear on the second panel, moderated by Marc, on Lovecraft's 'Life and Times'. After the other participants had spoken, Marc introduced Frank, who'd been parked in his wheelchair at the back of the auditorium. Stefan and Bob pushed him to the stage, followed closely by Lyda. While Frank and his chair were hauled into place, Lyda hoisted herself on the edge of the stage. "I am Lyda Arco Long," she announced, "Frank's attendant." She described his hospitalization the previous year – then proclaimed she was going to present a check for five hundred dollars to her great friend Brett. (I don't think Brett regretted having made a point of being out of town that weekend.) In the ensuing silence Marc turned the microphone over to Frank.

Frank had little to say other than to apologize for not being better prepared. "I'll do better next time," he said. "I'll now recite three poems." He didn't identify them, but I think one of the maybe two he did repeat was by Clark Ashton Smith. The audience clapped and cheered, at one point giving him a standing ovation. Afterwards, feeling bad about the distress my letter had caused Lyda, I went over to tell her how fitting I'd thought her remarks on Frank's health had been. She ignored me.

That evening Frank took part in one more panel, on the craft of the horror fiction writer, moderated by Bob and including a weary-looking Stefan. This time Frank brought a tattered page of notes that more than once he paused to consult with the aid of a magnifying glass. Unable to hear questions from the audience, he had to have Stefan repeat them in his ear. Again he received a big hand from the crowd, less for the content of his remarks than for his valiant effort to say anything at all half coherent. For those of us watching, especially the young for whom it was their first and probably last glimpse of the man, his very presence was enough. In response to a fellow panelist's request that he recite one of his own poems, Frank launched into 'The gods are dead...' Lyda was absent, decoyed by the promise of an interview.

Sunday morning I attended the panel of foreign experts. Julie pulled me out towards the end of it, saying Stefan wished to speak to me in the lobby. Lyda had gone berserk, Stefan reported. When he arrived to pick them up he found that she'd barricaded herself and Frank in their motel room and was screaming for their doctor. Frank was dying. She'd asked for me. I told Stefan there was probably nothing wrong, she was just being hysterical. Stefan rounded up some able bodies and returned to the motel. Julie said she'd learned that the night before, despite her failure to be interviewed (the 'interviewer' couldn't find the Days Inn), Lyda had accepted the situation calmly.

I returned to the auditorium for the final panel of the program, as a participant. My mother was in the audience, as were Julie and her parents. The last one to speak, I shared some thoughts on the current state of Lovecraft studies, which for all the achievements of recent years I said remained largely the province of amateur scholars, such as myself, and needed to attract more professionals, such as English professors, if Lovecraft was to gain wider recognition as a serious author. In his closing remarks, in an aside, ST said my call for more attention in the academy might do Lovecraft more harm than good. (Indeed, to let loose the deconstructionists and the multiculturalists on HPL would be no advance, yet in the long run I was confident he could only benefit if read and appreciated by literate people with more power and influence than ourselves.) During the question period Julie rose from her seat and challenged ST's dismissal of my argument. I was touched. Even after the end of the ceremonies she went up to ST and continued the debate.

When we got home to New York that evening we found an abusive message from Lyda on our machine. Julie exploded. At first she wanted to write the Longs a letter signed by me, then decided it was better simply to cease communication altogether. I had to agree. This was a step I'd been contemplating myself. We'd put up with their nonsense for far too long. I'd prided myself on my tolerance and patience. Where others had abandoned Frank when Lyda became too much to bear, I'd stuck it out. But now I was ready to leave Frank to his fate. After what I was sure had been his last hurrah, I was tired... One evening, while on our honeymoon in Sicily, Julie and I had dined at a restaurant with an outdoor garden. Suddenly the stillness was broken by the sound of broken crockery and a man shouting *"Basta!"* Enough. We stopped eating. We couldn't tell the source of the noise, but it had to be coming from one of the houses overlooking the garden. Seconds later there was another crash of crockery and again a masculine voice (that of a long-suffering husband who'd reached his limit?) shouted *"Basta!"* Smarting from Lyda's latest insult, I felt like that man. I'd had enough.

As it happened, Julie and I were moving at the end of August across the Hudson to Hoboken, New Jersey. With any luck the Longs would never find us there. Someone else could rummage through Frank's papers.

The next day Lyda phoned. She'd changed her tune – and was now offering me the check for five hundred dollars she originally announced she was giving Brett. As proof of my new determination, I hung up on her. I later spoke to Stefan, who told a harrowing tale of the drive home that Sunday morning. After managing to coax Lyda into unlocking the door to their motel room, he decided to get them back to New York as soon as possible. As a result of his self-sacrifice, Stefan had missed much of the conference and had scarcely enjoyed the part of it he did attend.

Later in the week Bob informed me that the Longs had been threatening to sue me because I hadn't hired a limousine to take them to Providence. They were puzzled they hadn't heard from Stefan since Sunday. Stefan was no doubt grateful they knew neither his phone number nor his last name. Bob also passed on the story that Frank had been proposing to a lot of women around the time he met Lyda. The wrong one just happened to accept. I told Bob and Stefan we'd severed relations with the Longs.

In September Stefan reported Lyda had written Kay that she and Frank were going to tour the Soviet Union with Gorbachev. In December Kay told me Lyda was back in one of her deep depressions. In January Lyda finally got our number in Hoboken. Julie listened long enough to hear her say Stephen King was giving them twenty-five thousand dollars and she was going to sue all us Lovecraftians. Or maybe she said Lousecraftians. A note from Kay said that Lyda couldn't understand why the Lovecraftians had dropped them. One day when I came home Julie said Lyda had called persistently. We considered getting an unlisted number.

XVIII

In the fall of '93 I spoke with Ted about ensuring Frank received an obituary in the *New York Times*. Though I hadn't seen Frank for more than three years, I did on occasion hear reports of his condition. Ben and Stefan had visited him recently in the hospital. The end had to be near. I unearthed a copy of Les Daniels' tribute, which Ted sent to the appropriate person at the *Times*. In the months following the centennial conference I'd picked up the paper every day half-expecting to read of Frank's death. But he'd continued to live on, ever weaker in body, mind, and spirit. Despite her having left me two years earlier for a fellow artist, I kept my word to Julie. Recovering from her loss was emotional trial enough without the added burden of resuming relations with the Longs. I was once again living in my old neighborhood on the Upper West Side – and had, as of that October, remarried.

The first Monday of the new year Ted called to say that Frank was dead. He'd died the day before, January 2, at St. Vincent's. Ted had heard the news from Kirby – he had no further details. Two days later the *New York Times* ran an obituary headed 'Frank Belknap Long, an Author of Science Fiction, Is Dead at 90,' accompanied by a photo dated 1949. Frank had been almost chubby in middle-age. The text clearly derived from Les Daniels' article. Ben phoned to say Lyda was okay. I wrote her a condolence letter.

The day after I mailed it I received a call from a woman with a Spanish accent, presumably a home attendant. Lyda was wondering how I'd found out about Frank. I wondered at the speed of the mail, and said I was available to visit anytime. Later Lyda herself left a message, a friendly one. When I stopped in that Saturday, I found all was forgiven. She remembered the time I'd left my own party in order to come stay with her. She never forgot a kindness.

I heard about Frank's last months. After a fall in which he broke three ribs, he went into the hospital where he ended up spending five weeks in the ward for, as she put, "the mildly psychotic." When he came home he wouldn't let anyone touch him and yelled obscenities. He complained that he was lonely, unable to understand why no one came to see him. Lyda apparently didn't know what if any arrangements had been made for his funeral. She gave me a letter from an official at Woodlawn Cemetery, dated the previous September, verifying that Frank was entitled to be buried in the Long family plot.

Later I spoke to Ted, Bob, and Stefan. No one seemed to know what was happening. I suggested we hold a memorial service at the grave in the spring. For the moment, Stefan told me, the hospital was willing to hold Frank's body in the morgue. At the end of January I received from Lyda what I later realized was a copy of the last page of a memorial tribute to Frank that Stefan had written for *Locus*, the *Time* or *Newsweek* of the science fiction field. On one side she'd penned, 'Come All Ye Faithful – I miss him so'; on the other, 'Recall – Peter – one night I asked you to stay – and you did – and how is the spouse – my best.'

In February I wrote a short story called 'The Letters of Halpin Chalmers', a sequel to 'The Hound of Tindalos', that conveyed my ambivalent feelings about Frank and Lyda far better perhaps (certainly more succinctly) than any lengthy memoir. Though it only marginally fit the genre, Stefan was kind enough to accept the tale for one of the Barnes & Nobles anthologies he'd been co-editing, *100 Crooked Little Crime Stories*. In March, while doing some free-lance work at the New York Public Library, I looked up Frank's birthdate on microfilm. The records showed a Frank B Long had been born in Manhattan on April 27, 1901, two years earlier than the usual date in the reference books.

In June I spoke to Kay. She and Kirby weren't taking the lead on arranging a funeral or memorial service, though they'd be glad to chip in if someone else did. I said I'd consider assuming the responsibility. Lyda continued to be abusive towards them. Since they'd sent out an appeal for money when Frank was in his last illness, donations for his burial were slow in coming from those in the science fiction world. Later in the month I spoke to Mark Berman, to whom the letter from Woodlawn Cemetery had been addressed. Though we'd never crossed paths, I gathered he'd looked after the Longs' day to day needs for years, buying food, running errands. His late mother had been Lyda's best friend.

Mark had some startling news – Frank had been buried months before in Potter's Field, where the city's indigent are unceremoniously laid to rest. "Don't tell Lyda I told you," he said. I should have known St. Vincent's wouldn't have held his body indefinitely. Happily, having read a *New Yorker* article on Potter's Field, I knew the process wasn't irreversible. Mark said he'd received an estimate of $2,100 to have Frank exhumed and reburied. (By keeping him on ice, Lyda had been hoping to continue receiving his Social Security payments.) I told Mark I thought this sum could be raised within the larger Lovecraftian community.

On a hot day in early summer Ben and I paid Lyda a call. As Mark had warned, she was in one of her manic phases. "Wait a minute," she shouted from behind the door. "I'm naked!" Lyda herself greeted us, wrapped in a sheet. "Ben and Peter, my two favorite people!" she exclaimed. "Thank God, thank God." We followed her into the living room, where she sat on the bed, cooled by two small electric fans. We saw no home attendant. In response to some ribald comment from Lyda, Ben joked about his sex life after a prostate operation. He knew exactly how to handle her – by being playful, by refusing to take offence at any of her more personal remarks. Lyda loved it. For my part I was concerned to avert my eyes as her casually draped sheet didn't always preserve modesty. Attempts to discuss retrieving Frank from Potter's Field were unavailing.

In July Mara Kirk Hart, daughter of George Kirk, one of the original Kalems, came to town. A librarian, she'd run across *Pulptime* (in which her father has a bit part) and written me early in '91 inquiring about other members of the Kalem Club. I'd replied that Frank was to the best of my knowledge the group's only survivor. We'd met the summer of '93 in New York, and now she was back for another visit, with her grown daughter. One evening, as I later heard, the two of them spent five hours with Lyda. They ordered take-out food, they gossiped, they had a hilarious time. Mara mentioned Nan, my new wife, whose existence I'd been keeping a secret from Lyda. Now that we were back in touch, I feared the prospect of her becoming fixated on Nan, as well as her probing me about a painful recent past. Nonetheless, I was glad that Mara had been the one to inform her of this dramatic change in my own life.

In August Lyda mailed me photocopy blow-ups of two pictures – one of the Polaroid shot of me and their dog with Frank to the side, the other of a long ago party in their living room, filled with smartly dressed men and women. In the surrounding white space she'd written the names of a few of the guests – Paul Destinée, George Reavey, Yvette Chantilly – everyone a musician or an artist. In September she sent me a Jewish New Year's card, or to be precise, a photocopy of Tenniel's white rabbit from *Alice in Wonderland* bearing a banner with 'best of years' wishes from 'Lydash and Frankele'.

As part of his fall Necronomicon Press catalogue, Marc included an appeal for funds to pay for Frank's burial in Woodlawn Cemetery. He discreetly didn't mention that Frank, for the moment at least, was planted in Potter's Field. The fans on Marc's mailing list were quick to respond. Stephen King gave most generously. By the end of the month Marc had received enough money for us to proceed.

When I visited the funeral home on West 23rd where Mark had gotten the original estimate, I discovered that complete costs would run to more than three thousand dollars. Annoying, but an amount still within the capacity of Necronomicon Press to raise. Bob agreed to come in from New Jersey to officiate at a memorial service, which we set for three in the afternoon of November 3, a Thursday. That Frank might not be in Woodlawn by that date I decided didn't matter, as long as we knew he was on his way. I brought the papers to authorize the transfer over to Lyda, who for once was in a mood to cooperate. Indeed, she was humbly grateful for our efforts. Since she hadn't been feeling well, she told me to go as soon as she'd signed the papers. Marc sent the funeral home a $2,100 check, the rest to be paid on delivery.

I ordered a map from Woodlawn that turned out to include a history with a list of famous occupants. Founded in 1863, the Woodlawn Cemetery billed itself as the second oldest organization in the Bronx. Under the 'Hall of Fame' category labeled 'Famous Writers, Poets, Etc.' were, among other illustrious names, Herman Melville and Countee Cullen. Frank would be in good company. Perhaps one day an updated version would mention the author of 'The Space Eaters' and 'The Hounds of Tindalos'.

I spoke to Kay, who promised to provide champagne and flowers for the reception tentatively scheduled after the ceremony. Before the end of October, however, both Mark and Ben informed me that Lyda was too ill either to attend the service or receive visitors at home – she might even have to check into the hospital. A pity she couldn't make an event where she deserved to be center stage, but then her absence meant less trouble for others.

The afternoon of November 3, I drove Ted up to the Bronx and promptly got lost. We arrived at Woodlawn ten minutes after the hour to find that those ahead of us had yet to locate the Long family plot. From the cemetery map, though, we knew we had to be close. After some assiduous hunting I discovered the tall granite obelisk that I knew had to be nearby, marked on one of its four sides with the names of Frank's grandparents. We reassembled by this monument, fifteen or so of us, including Stefan, Scott, and ST.

Under a low, bright autumn sun, dressed in full clerical garb, Bob conducted an informal service as befit Frank's agnostic beliefs, reading poems by both the deceased and his friend HPL. When Bob called for people to step forward and share their thoughts, three did so. One was Joe Wrzos, former editor of *Amazing*, a magazine that had published Frank back in the days when his stories still had a professional market. Another was Ben. The third was Perry Grayson, not yet twenty-one, who'd flown from California just for the occasion. Perry regarded Frank as his literary idol. I took photographs. The group broke up around four. I drove a carfull of passengers back to Manhattan via the teeming streets of the South Bronx, having somehow missed the turn-off for the highway.

The following week Mark called to tell me that Lyda was in the hospital, with liver and pancreatic cancer. She might have only months or weeks to live. As it turned out, when I stopped by St. Vincent's the next evening, she had less time than that. When I first entered her room I mistook another old woman for her. In fact, Lyda was in the bed opposite, heavily sedated, almost unrecognizable with an oxygen mask over her nose and mouth. She may have turned her head slightly towards me when I spoke, but I doubted she recognized me. In the hall I found a nurse, who explained that that morning Lyda had made a fuss – torn at her IV, screamed and cursed the doctor. I could imagine. So instead of the hospice route, she ended up on a morphine drip. Instead of a couple more weeks of life, she now had only a couple more days. Relieved of her suffering, she would never regain consciousness.

Outside the hospital, as I walked the few blocks east to the restaurant where I was meeting Nan for dinner, I shed a few tears. I was sad in a way I simply hadn't been when I heard the news of Frank's death. For Frank I'd felt mainly relief that he was at last out of his misery. For Lyda I felt genuine sorrow. I regretted that I hadn't told her of my doings during the years of my silence – for in the end I realized that, as mean and selfish and crazy as she could be, she'd appreciated who I was and what I had done for them and, unlike Frank, had told me so. And with her passing, too, I was mourning a part of my life forever gone yet from which I was hurrying with a sense of renewed hope and joy.

XIX

Early in the afternoon, two days later, four of us met on the stoop of 421 West 21st Street – myself, Ben, Mark, and a stranger named Brad. Ben and I decided later that Mark must have alerted Brad that the moment had come to check the Longs' apartment for valuables. Brad said he was an old friend of Frank's. A graduate student in theology at Princeton, this young man admitted he was also a book collector and dealer.

Mark let us into the building and the apartment with his keys. I made a point of telling Mark that we regarded him as Lyda's heir, that anything of hers after her death belonged to him. Since Lyda was sure to have no will, I was of course acting outside the law. In the circumstances, however, both Ben and I felt this was a morally justified gesture, one worthy of Sherlock Holmes himself. Mark thanked me.

Once inside Brad announced that Lyda had promised he could have Frank's Life Achievement Award. A cast-metal effigy of HP Lovecraft designed by the cartoonist Gahan Wilson, the 'Howard' was the horror world's equivalent of the Oscar. Neither Ben nor I objected. What did we know? Mark, not being an aficionado of the genre, was in no position to judge. Brad secured his trophy in the living room.

The living room looked almost abandoned – dustier and more paper strewn than it had been my last visit. From a desk Mark pulled out Lyda's passport, which he said he'd used in repeated and fruitless efforts to get her on Medicaid. From the same desk Mark retrieved some old snapshots. One tattered print, dated February 1958, showed a red-haired, red-lipped Lyda before a fireplace in a golden, off-the-shoulder gown. Between the fingers of one red-nailed hand lifted to the mantel was an aperitif glass half filled with red liquid. On the back she'd written 'The Jade of Jades (the mask of sophistication)' and 'Lyda not Lydasha'. Mark confirmed that the apartment had been hers at the time she and Frank were married. She'd probably been living there since the forties. Despite her claims of multiple husbands, she'd had only one. As for her singing career, she had once sung a solo as part of a program at Carnegie Recital Hall.

The next stop was Frank's bedroom, the last mystery. For years I'd wondered what it contained, though I wasn't expecting to find much of interest. In the event, I was in for a pleasant surprise. There was a bureau, a desk, a single bed beneath the lone security-fenced window – and dozens and dozens of books, heaped here and there. Frank's horror library occupied a set of shelves at the head of his bed. While he'd long before sold such rarities as *The Outsider*, Lovecraft's first Arkham House collection, he still had plenty of books that fans would want, including battered paperback copies of the Gothics he'd penned under Lyda's name and such later novels as *Monster from Out of Time* and *The Night of the Wolf*. There was a stack of his chapbook, *Rehearsal Night*. Brad, who knew his way around the bedroom from past visits, encouraged Ben and me to help ourselves.

And help myself I did, like the proverbial kid let loose in the candy shop. Chief among my acquisitions for my own library were a jacketless copy of *The Early Long* and a beat-up Arkham House edition of *The Hounds of Tindalos*. Greedy I may have been, but given the poor condition of virtually every volume I was hardly enriching myself. Frank, I liked to think, would have wanted me to have a book or two or three of his, had he for a moment thought to stop his nit-picking and show me some gratitude. Furthermore, others not present who'd been true friends to the Longs deserved some tangible reward. Certain items I set aside in my mind for these selfless souls.

Brad suggested I might like to take Frank's typewriter (there was only one), but I didn't need a bulky old manual typewriter. Another relic Brad brought to my attention, however, did catch my fancy – the manuscript of what must have been the novel Frank said for years he was working on and never completed, *Cottage Tenant*. It could in fact be a scarce example of a Long manuscript, for the trunk full of Frank's papers Lyda had asked me to go through was nowhere to be found. Brad had seen it in recent years, but it wasn't in its accustomed spot.

We inspected another trunk, which contained ordinary books – contemporary thrillers, a bestseller or two – nonetheless reflecting some literary taste. One title caught my eye, an old paperback of Dostoevsky's *The Idiot*. There were boxes too. One held a collection of old vinyl records, 78s – classical, heavy on opera. Another was filled with Yiddish theater memorabilia. Brad promised to take this material to the Yivo Center for Jewish Research. On the floor were a couple of scraps of paper of personal relevance – a postal card I'd sent Frank thanking him for his introductory comments on my Lovecraft study; a royalty statement from Paul Ganley for one or two dollars, Frank's annual share of *Pulptime*.

A home attendant arrived. She looked sad, no doubt aware that Lyda wouldn't be coming home. We told her to take anything she wanted from the living room and kitchen. As for the books, Ben and I were fast formulating a plan. Even with the cream skimmed off the top, Frank's library could, we reckoned, bring hundreds of dollars. More money was needed to pay the total cost of his reburial. Having his name engraved on the family monument in Woodlawn would be an additional expense. Ben suggested we take the books to a dealer he knew upstate. I had a better idea – why not ship them to Marc in Rhode Island? He could prepare a catalogue and offer the collection to the patrons of Necronomicon Press. They after all had been among Frank's more loyal supporters in his last years, buying his *Autobiographical Memoir* and issues of *Crypt* featuring his fiction. They deserved first crack at a souvenir from the library of Frank Belknap Long.

With Mark's approval, Ben and I relayed armfuls of books into his capacious station wagon parked on the street. We had no time to waste finding boxes to pack them in first. By mid-afternoon we'd finished loading every book we figured Frank's fans would consider significant. We were ready to leave but not so Brad, who was in a panic. He couldn't find the Howard. Ben and I were perplexed. What could have happened to it? After a few minutes we discovered the home attendant was the unwitting culprit. From the bottom of a garbage bag she'd been packing full of old clothes and costume jewelry, she produced the statuette. Brad's relief at recovering his prize was palpable.

Ben and I drove over to St. Vincent's, where we found Lyda still in a coma. We tried to discover what would happen to her when she died, but no one could answer us since in theory only a family member could deal with the matter. Ben had already learned that the cost of having her cremated would be around four hundred dollars. Back home I found a message on my machine from the undertaker handling Frank's reburial that it was set for Wednesday, two days hence. That evening I phoned Marc Michaud. He said he'd be glad to handle the disposal of Frank's library through Necronomicon Press. Later that night Mark Berman called to tell me he'd heard from the hospital – Lyda was dead.

XX

The next day I brought Ted up to date. I was confident no one would challenge our removing Frank's books – the stakes were too small. His literary estate was highly unlikely to generate the kind of money to provoke legal wrangling.

"I guess you haven't heard," said Ted. "Steven Spielberg has just announced plans to film 'The Hounds of Tindalos'."

I laughed, but not for long. The following morning I heard from the funeral home that we had to reschedule for Thursday. Because of unrest on Riker's Island the prisoners were locked up in their cells that day and couldn't do any digging in Potter's Field. Then Ben phoned with worse news. Mark had just learned that since Lyda died intestate we had no right to clean out the apartment. The contents belonged to the city. Not wanting to break the law, Ben was prepared to give all the books back.

I spoke to Mark. He was seeing somebody downtown about the matter that afternoon. He was hopeful that we wouldn't have to turn over everything we'd collected on Monday to the authorities. He agreed not to make a point of admitting we'd taken books that were of some value. He would, however, be honest. Like Ben, he was inclined to stick to the letter of the law. When I said he was the one who stood to lose the most, he said he'd have to accept that. (Of course, the other big losers would be the collectors of Longiana.)

While I didn't say so to my fellow thieves, I for my part wasn't about to surrender any of my Long goodies to the city, especially not the manuscript of *Cottage Tenant*, which I now took the time to examine more closely. It consisted of two partial drafts, mostly photocopied pages. The first couple of paragraphs afforded a unique glimpse of Frank as wordsmith, starting with the first, handwritten draft.

Chapter one opened on a lyrical note: 'Of all American shorelines the Coast of New England appears to have been the most mysteriously haunted. Dreamers, visionaries, poets and prophets have made of it a time-dissolving portal into the unknown close to without precedent.' My editorial eye halted at that final prepositional phrase. How about 'close to unprecedented' or 'almost unprecedented' – or better yet, why not end the sentence after the word 'unknown'? Well, that would have spoiled the rhythm. The phrase 'close to without precedent', after all, did sound poetic. Hence it remained in the second, typed draft.

The second paragraph of the first draft resumed: 'Thoreau, the most legendary of hermits, spent a lengthy period attached to the blowing sands of Cape Cod's desolate wasteland, Hawthorne described its periph[er]ies as a magnet for witches, and Melville in a miraculous display of genius, hovered over a captain and crew that went white whaling in a several-times-repeated screen dramatization.' Huh? It must have taken a miraculous display of genius to make those screen dramatizations seaworthy, particularly the several-times-repeated variety.

In the second draft, no doubt mindful of the need to revise, Frank had let Melville hover 'over a captain and crew that went white whaling in a famous screen dramatization by Ray Bradbury.' Well, this was an improvement. As far as I knew *Moby-Dick* had been made into a movie only once. Sensing perhaps that he still didn't have it right, Frank had crossed out the end of the sentence so that in the final version the captain and crew go 'white whaling in a Moby Dicksonian legend that transcends its creator.' Were those echoes of Emily Dickinson and Transcendentalism deliberate, I wondered? A perusal of *Cottage Tenant* after the first page confirmed that Frank's failure to complete his last novel was no tragedy.

That evening I spoke to Mark again. All was well. The city bureaucrats weren't about to insist we return what we took from the Longs' apartment. Ben was willing to proceed as originally planned with shipping Frank's books to Marc in Rhode Island.

The next day, before meeting ST for the drive up to the Bronx, I went by the apartment for a final sweep. Mark had given me his set of keys on Monday. The place looked all the more desolate, ransacked. I didn't envy the landlord. It might be a while before the premises were cleaned up and available for rental. I looked in vain for Frank's HWA award and had to presume Brad had taken it as well as the Howard. And what of the painting of Lyda and the swan? Would whoever finally unscrewed it from the wall bother to save it? I salvaged a few more paperbacks, in particular the copy of *The Idiot* I'd spotted in the trunk. It turned out to be inscribed: 'To my Beloved "Idiot"! Lyda Long'. Perhaps she'd given it to Frank as a wedding present. (Dostoevsky's 'idiot' is Prince Myshkin, a naively open, child-like man too good for the corrupt society that eventually destroys him, I later discovered on reading the novel.)

I stopped at the funeral home on West 23rd, where I made sure the prisoners at Riker's were cooperating that day and I had proper directions. I delivered a check for the balance. After rendezvousing with ST, we bought sandwiches at a deli and headed up to Woodlawn. There, at one o'clock by the main entrance, we met Fred, the funeral director I'd been dealing with, in his station wagon. I could have ordered a hearse to transport the body – no doubt Frank and Lyda would have preferred him to travel in style on his final earthly journey – but as neither was in a position to object I had as usual chosen to go economy.

A car supplied by the cemetery led our little procession to the grave site, where Ben was waiting. The sky was gray and overcast, the temperature more fall-like than it had been two weeks before at the memorial service. Under Fred's supervision a work crew unloaded the metallic bronze casket (in theory the cheapest model) and placed it on the bier, while I took pictures. Did that casket really contain Frank's remains? What if it was the wrong body – say, that of a poor anonymous black person? Maybe earlier I should have asked to verify the identity of the corpse in its wooden box when it was delivered to the funeral home, but my taste for the ghoulish didn't extend beyond the printed page. I was content to trust the *New Yorker* article's assertion that those in charge kept excellent records at Potter's Field.

I photographed Ben and ST by the casket, then handed my camera to Ben for him to take my picture at the same spot. At last Fred suggested it would be appropriate for one of us to say a few words. Addressing myself mainly to the solemn workmen standing at a respectful distance, I explained that we'd already had a service for Frank and that he was finally where he belonged. The three of us continued to chat among ourselves, until I realized we were keeping the workmen from finishing their job. We moved on, in search of Lovecraft's grandparents' grave. We found the headstone, almost hidden by an overgrown bush. I snapped a picture of Ben and ST holding back the branches so as to reveal the name 'Lovecraft'.

The next day I spoke to Brett, who'd moved back to New York. He said he'd persuaded Lyda not to throw out a cache of Frank's papers, though it appeared at some point she did so, perhaps when Frank was in the hospital during his final illness. I mailed the *Cottage Tenant* manuscript to Marc, who listed it in his catalogue of the Frank Belknap Long library. At $250 it was more than ten times the price of the average item offered. Sales from the catalogue paid for all funeral-related expenses, including Lyda's cremation, which occurred the same day as Frank's reburial.

In January I received a letter, dated November 17, from Brad, who'd originally mailed it to my old, pre-Hoboken address. Among other evidence of his efforts on Lyda's behalf, Brad enclosed a copy of the cover letter he'd sent to an individual at the Yivo Center along with Lyda's vital papers on her family and the Yiddish theater. He suggested that they call Mark Berman to arrange for the removal of the painting in the Longs' hall. He identified the artist as Haile Hendrix, a cartoonist, and two of the other figures in the painting as the author Bel Kaufman and the actress Bette Davis. Perhaps within her own realm, I fleetingly thought, Lyda had left a greater legacy than Frank had in his field.

Also in the new year Perry invited me to contribute to a booklet of articles he was editing about Frank's life and work. Perry would indeed found his own small press devoted largely to publishing work by and about Lovecraft's best friends. At the Lunacon in March I bought a copy of Frank's story-cycle-turned-novel, *John Carstairs: Space Detective*. I was becoming a casual Long collector. I contracted with a stone-cutter to have his full name and dates inscribed on the family obelisk. This would fill the available space. When asked, I said Frank's widow would not be joining him in Woodlawn. I wasn't quite telling the truth.

By what would have been Frank's ninety-fourth birthday, when Ben and I returned to Woodlawn, the engraving was finished. Ben supplied yarmulkes and recited the Kaddish. I read the translation of the Hebrew in phonetic English as best I could. Over Frank's sunken, not yet grass-covered grave we took turns sprinkling Lyda's ashes – half of them at any rate. Mark had reserved the other half for casting into the waters off Seagate, in Brooklyn. (In her last days, according to Mark, Lyda had expressed the wish at one point to be with her beloved husband, at another to become one with the ocean opposite her favorite part of Brooklyn.) That ceremony, however, I wasn't planning to attend. I'd performed my last service for those 'old, dear, exasperating, maddening but unique friends', to borrow Ben's phrase from the affectionate memoir of the Longs he would prepare for his EOD zine. I was free – free to begin contemplating writing my own memoir of that immortal couple.

Afterword

Ramsey Campbell

I have frequently discovered myself to be of the opinion, which I have not been shy of expressing aloud even if there was nobody else to hear – though I'm assuming, of course, the total absence on these occasions of invisible spectres and of any other presences not discernible to ordinary eyes – that an account of the last years of Frank and Lyda Long ought to be set down for the record by somebody who not only knew them but who is in possession of sufficient talent for prose to do them justice – a writer, in other words, unless some tentacled denizen of another planet in orbit around, let us say, distant Betelgeuse could be found to have observed them in the apartment where they ultimately lived and was able to share the experience. Such a one (I leave my readers to decide on his humanity or otherwise) is Peter Cannon. In case anybody who has read up to this point is wondering whether his memoir is exaggerated, let me say that my experience suggests it couldn't be. Jenny and I often reminisce about the evening we spent with the Longs.

It was in 1976, after the World Fantasy Convention in New York. The Longs were at the convention, Frank pottering about for all the world like a Brooklyn version of the Walter Brennan character in *Rio Bravo*. Lyda summoned us to their table in the hotel lounge and greeted me as (apparently Frank's phrase) a brilliant young writer. She invited us to dine at their apartment, promising that we would eat as we had never eaten before. Indeed, our first stay in New York was to be marked by unforgettable meals – this was the convention at which the banquet proved to be a buffet delivered in meagre servings at yawning intervals, all of which maddened the famished fans, who swooped on it like vultures onto carrion. Eventually one dissatisfied banqueter went out and bought a portion of Kentucky Fried Chicken to fling at the convention committee. At the time we saw none of this as an omen of dinner with the Longs.

Kirby McCauley was invited, but pleaded a previous engagement. I'm not sure whether it was on his recommendation that we took a litre of white wine with us – a wise move, at any rate. We arrived on time, to find that for some reason nobody else had. Frank ushered us past a bicycle into the bedroom Peter has already immortalised, then took refuge in the bathroom. "Frank, you bastard," Lyda screeched to make him vacate it. "Where have you put my tiara? He's being a prima donna in there." She continued to assure us how uniquely we would eat. Eventually some of our fellow guests ventured to appear – Ben and Janet Indick, H Warner Munn and his young companion Brenda, who had been thoughtful enough to bring a joint we young folks duly smoked next to the bicycle. I can't remember the names of the other guests, but the place soon took on all the qualities of a party in the heyday of the beat generation, or perhaps a version of one dreamed up by Hollywood. A stringy fellow sang or intoned – even at the time it was impossible to judge – poems while accompanying himself on a guitar. A later arrival than most, a spectacularly neurotic young woman, said nothing for several hours before without any visible preamble she downed most of a bottle of vodka and passed out on the bed. Perhaps she had been overcome by the tardy spectacle of the promised dinner: half a baked potato per guest, to accompany their portion of the piece de resistance, a silver salver bearing an artistic arrangement of four hot dogs surrounding segments of not as many more. It did tempt Frank out of the bathroom. Presumably he spoke to the guests, but it's Lyda we recall. Attired not in a tiara but a kaftan, she told Jenny how, having been brought up in India, she spoke proper English like us but unlike Frank.

You can take all this as being horribly funny or horribly sad – more likely both. I just wish I could offer more to balance it, but I don't think it helped Frank that his early work became legendary in his lifetime. Certainly *The Hounds of Tindalos* used to be a favourite book of mine, so that when he sent me a story for *New Tales of the Cthulhu_Mythos* I could hardly wait to read it – not, at least, until I saw the first line: "It was just the right place for an encounter with an enchantress." I imagine Lovecraft's reaction, had he been able to read that, might have been similar to mine – a sinking sense that Frank had lost his feeling for the tale of terror to the romances he'd written under his wife's name. The story tells how the narrator meets an attractive widow and her children on a beach, and talks to her about child-rearing and poetry. Eventually, maybe before the reader despairs, a Cthulhoid item floats, up and sinks again. I waited for a punch line but found none, and so suggested a final paragraph to Frank, which he said I should add to the story myself. He did, however, assure me that it was one of his strongest stories.

It wasn't, and that, more than the encounter with him and Lyda, is why Frank haunts me. Just as Peter and his wife saw their own potential future in the Longs, I often wonder if I'm as wrong as Frank to feel that my work is improving. Sometimes only the fact that I'm able to imagine the dread possibility is a reassurance. Poor Frank! Poor Lyda! At least they've entertained us in their way, and Frank left us images that enrich the imagination. I shall continue to remember the long hand the space-eaters reached into the forest, a glimpse worthy of Lovecraft and his praise, and try not to be too hard on the shakier passages of the tale. The pulps would have been poorer without Frank, and so would my waking dreams. If I can see no point in telling less than the truth as I know it, certainly part of that truth is that I was enthralled by his work when I was learning the tradition of my field, and was privileged to meet him.

Ramsey Campbell
Wallasey, Merseyside
July 1997

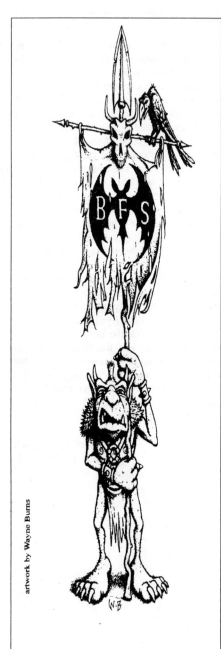

artwork by Wayne Burns

There is a group of people who know all the latest publishing news and gossip. They enjoy the very best in fiction from some of the hottest talents around. They can also read articles by and about their favourite authors and know in advance when those authors' books are being published.

These people belong to the
British Fantasy Society.

The BFS publishes a regular newsletter, *Prism UK*, as well as numerous magazines and booklets containing fantasy, horror and science fiction, speculative articles, artwork, reviews, interviews, comment and much more. They also organise the acclaimed annual Fantasycon, the British Fantasy Convention, to which publishers, editors and authors flock to hear the announcement of the coveted British Fantasy Awards, voted on by the members.

Membership of the British Fantasy Society is open to everyone. The annual UK subscription is £17.00, which covers the newsletter and magazines. Overseas membership: £20.00 Europe, $35.00 USA, £25 elsewhere.

To join, send monies payable to 'The British Fantasy Society' , together with your name and address, to:

The BFS Secretary, 2 Harwood Street,
Stockport, SK4 1JJ, UK.

Visit our Web site:
http://www.djb.u-net.com